YOU'RE OUR CHILD

A Social/Psychological
Approach to Adoption

Jerome Smith
Indiana University
and

Franklin I. Miroff

Foreword by
Beulah R. Compton

UNIVERSITY
PRESS OF
AMERICA

LANHAM • NEW YORK • LONDON

Copyright © 1981 by

University Press of America,™ Inc.

4720 Boston Way
Lanham, MD 20706

3 Henrietta Street
London WC2E 8LU England

Library of Congress Cataloging in Publication Data

Smith, Jerome.
        You're our child.

        Bibliography: p.
        Includes index.
        1. Adoption–United States. 2. Children, Adopted–
United States–Family relationships. 3. Adoption–United
States–Psychological aspects. I. Miroff, Franklin I., joint
author. II. Title.
HV875.S624   362.7'34'0973   80–5957
        ISBN 0–8191–1416–2
        ISBN 0–8191–1417–0 (pbk.)

FOREWORD

It is with pleasure that I respond to the request that I contribute a foreword to this book. I warmly recommend the book to adoptive parents and to couples considering adoption; to those who want to understand the meaning of adoption; to adoptive parents and adopted children; and to professionals who work with those who either seek to adopt children or who are adoptive parents. Written by a social worker and an attorney, both of whom are themselves adoptive parents, it makes an important contribution to the understanding of the feelings of adoptive parents and adopted children. It deals with their relationships to each other and to the world outside the family, that is often thoughtlessly cruel in the way it responds to such families and their members.

You're Our Child is a unique book in that it speaks in a realistic way to the commonness of all parenting experiences and all child development struggles, while at the same time recognizing the meaning for adoptive parents and their children found in the reality of fact that the family began through a legal process rather than through a biological birth process. It accepts neither the notion that the rejection of a child by its birth parents is a determining factor that colors all the rest of life, nor the notion that the problems and questions of the adopted child can be adequately dealt with by the story of the "chosen child." The focus of the book is clearly on the reality of adoption as an element of family functioning that adds a certain complexity to the normal family processes, neither to be denied nor overemphasized. Thus it offers to adoptive parents helpful information not available in other literature on adoption.

For the social worker, attorney, doctor, judge or other professional who works with adoptive parents, the book offers a unique opportunity to develop a sensitivity to the meaning of adoption in a family's life, and to the ways adopted children and their parents are often discriminated against by professional people. It should offer a social worker a realistic understanding of some of the emotional issues an adoptive parent or an adopted child must confront in building a satisfying parent-child relationship. No other book so clearly introduces professionals to the meaning of adoption in family life. It should be thoughtfully read by all who deal with the adoptive process.

Beulah Roberts Compton

Indiana University

ACKNOWLEDGMENTS

There are many individuals who have contributed significantly to the writing of this book. For substantive contributions, we are indebted to the following persons: Marcia Velders, Mary McKinney Lett and Lisa Stine. Special thanks go to four young women whose editing led to substantially greater clarity, and without whose contributions the completion of this book would not have been possible: Joy Newell, Rebecca Speulda, Sally Cook Sider and Jennifer Joyce.

To our wifes, Inez Smith and Roberta Miroff, we are particularly grateful for their constant support and encouragement. For typing and technical assistance, we owe a debt of thanks to Janice Forthman and Jan Hill.

Finally, we come to those principals about whom this book is written. We dedicate the book to our children, both adopted and biological, who gave us the inspiration to write: Sandy, Bobby, Laura, Andrew and Debbie -- simply because they are all our children.

TABLE OF CONTENTS

PREFACE

Parents everywhere share so much in common that the need for a special guide for adoptive parents might not be readily apparent. Legally, the ties established through adoption are equivalent to biological ties, carrying with them the same expectations, rights and privileges shared by any other set of biological parents. This view holds that parenthood is parenthood and the law makes no distinction between parenthood by adoption and parenthood by procreation.

Nevertheless, adoption does give rise to unique life situations which should be recognized as such and dealt with accordingly. Certainly the legal distinction between the two aforementioned types of parenthood is clear enough: Adoption involves the transferring of rights and responsibilities of birth parents to other adults who have had no previous legal obligations to the child. Beyond the legalities of adoption, there extend far-reaching social, emotional and psychological attitudes and consequences which figure greatly in the life situations created by adoption.

It is the primary purpose of this book to identify these other factors which affect most families who adopt a child today, factors which to date have not been explored in depth in the literature. We will examine them as they derive from society and the law, and as they relate to the adoptive parent and the adopted child. The book deals primarily with the most prevalent adoptive form: A healthy infant adopted soon after birth by a married couple of the same race as the child.

This book is an outgrowth of an observation that books on adoptive parenting are unavailable.

A comprehensive search of the literature reveals that what is available generally falls into one of two categories. The first category treats the subject in a simplistic fashion. These books recommend warm and accepting ways of telling the story to the child of how he or she came to live with you. There is a storybook flavor apparent, and the reader comes away believing that "they all lived happily ever after." While such a book may have some merit in first explaining adoption to a toddler, it is our view that it is simply not enough. The second category of books on the adoptive experience is at the highly theoretical level. These books suggest that the adopted child's growth is thwarted because, by being exposed to the knowledge that he was once given up, he experiences a rejection and humiliation from which he may never fully psychologically recover. Such a position is rooted in a body of knowledge and suppositions deriving from psychoanalytic theory. There is reason to question the validity of this view. In fact, research findings seem to suggest that the adopted child reacts more to the way adoption is handled than to the fact of adoption. Therefore, to an adoptive parent, the theory is limited, at best, in its application and usefulness.

The terminology in the book merits comment. In this book, adoptive parents are referred to either as adoptive parents or as adopters. Adopted children are referred to either as adopted children or as adoptees. For purposes of clarification, we will refer to parents who keep children born to them as biological parents. Persons who relinquish their children for purposes of adoption will be referred to as birth parents.

The data for the book are drawn from the personal and professional experiences of the authors,

both of whom are adoptive parents. Jerome Smith
is a clinical social worker-educator who is an
associate professor at the Indiana University
School of Social Work, Indianapolis, Indiana. He
is a clinical consultant at Catholic Social Services in Indianapolis. He has had extensive experience as a family therapist and adoption agency
administrator. He and his wife have three children,
two of whom are adopted. Franklin Miroff is an
attorney in private practice in the Indianapolis
area who has represented numerous couples in adoption
proceedings. He and his wife have two adopted children. The authors work together in providing adoptive
parent counseling to new adopters and have conducted
group meetings on this subject at the Jewish Community
Center at Indianapolis. It was from this joint experience that the need was recognized for writing this
book.

The title of the book is deliberate. All too frequently, adoptive parents hear remarks from others
about the child's "real" parentage. Recently a book
was published under the title Somebody Else's Child
(Silman, 1976). Inasmuch as the major task for adoptive parents is to develop the feeling that their
adopted child is really and truly their own child, we
felt it appropriate to reflect that view in the title:
You're Our Child.

CHAPTER I

ADOPTION -- THE EVOLVING SCENE

The human existence does not occur in a vacuum for individuals and families. All people are somehow influenced by the trends and traditions evolving during their lifetime in the society in which they live and of which they are a part. Adoptive parents and children are no exception to this general rule. Indeed, they are uniquely vulnerable to the vicissitudes of societal attitudes towards them. The parents' success in rearing a happy and healthy child may be placed in jeopardy by the behavior of relatives (whether they be grandparents, aunts, uncles and siblings), friends, neighbors, or even casual acquaintances. They are also influenced by comments made by teachers, clergy, doctors, social workers and lawyers with whom the parents and children come into contact during their lifetime. Even opportunities to adopt are dependent upon legal authorities, social agencies and, of course, birth parents.

This book, therefore, begins with an examination of the background factors affecting adoption today. The adoption picture in the United States is changing significantly. Currently, it is in a state of flux and uncertainty. Changes are evident in the pattern of adoption and in attitudes toward it. Some of these changes seemingly affect only one participant in the process. Most changes, however, have an impact upon them all.

A traditional adoption myth, based partly on a historical perspective, revolves around an abandoned or orphaned child rescued from desperate circumstances by a charitable couple. Reflecting society's social Darwinistic view of fitness,

1

meaning that some children were more fit than others, social agencies became quite restrictive and selective and consequently developed the concept of the "blue ribbon" baby as the most suitable child for adoption. The child may have been selected (in some cases by the prospective adoptive parents) from a group of infants residing in a foster home or a nursery. It is doubtful that this myth portrayed the realities of the typical adoption and most certainly has nothing in common with the realities of today.

There has been a pronounced decline in the availability of healthy, white infants for adoption. The decline has been so significant as to force social agencies, heretofore predominantly dependent on adoptive placement as a principal professional service, to seek other professional service functions. As recently as ten years ago, most people hoping to adopt a child found a healthy white infant after waiting only a brief period of time. Today a couple may wait years before their name reaches the top of the waiting list maintained by an adoption agency or attorney.

Several factors contribute to this dramatic change. First, and perhaps most important, the majority of children born out of wedlock are kept by one of the biological parents or their families. In the past an unmarried pregnant adolescent found that she had no other choice than to place the child for adoption. She now finds that keeping the child is a viable alternative. Second, the increased use of preventive birth control measures has presumably lowered the birth rate, although there is no way of knowing how many pregnancies were actually prevented through the use of contraceptives. Third, the increased availability of abortion has decreased the number of children who presumably would have been placed for adoption. Finally, the decision to place or not to place may be influenced by the perceived notion that many adoptees are seeking their birth parents. Certainly, one cannot guarantee anonymity and privacy in an atmosphere which includes a public clamor and outcry for the opening of sealed records. Hence, a birth mother may decide to either keep a child or abort in an effort to avoid such disclosure later in her life. The multiple impact of all these factors has tightened the market on children available for adoption. There is no indication, further, whether this trend will continue or reverse itself.

Whatever the causes, the effect upon adoptive parents is to eliminate the notion that they are the rescuers. They may feel, instead, that the child rescued them from a perpetual state of childlessness. Their long waiting period provides them with ample opportunity to make a deliberate choice to be parents; however, they do not choose their baby any more than biological parents do.

This is not to say that the traditional myth does not continue to contain a germ of truth. There remain many children awaiting adoption -- older children, children with mental and physical handicaps, and non-white or biracial children of all ages. The adoption of these children poses substantially different problems from that of the healthy newborn of the same race as his adoptive parents.

An extended discussion of these problems and proposed solutions is beyond the scope of this book. However, the existence of these children cannot be overlooked entirely. Couples seeking to adopt a healthy infant are advised of the availability of these other groups of children and

subsequently consider the option of adopting one
of these hard-to-place children. Although most
choose not to undertake this special challenge,
the fact that they do consider it may contribute
to a sense of having chosen their child. In this
sense, they do make a choice.

The contemporary scene contains other changes
as well. In the past, the beginning of the parent-
child relationship differed markedly from that of
biological parenthood. As previously noted, only
the healthiest babies were considered adoptable.
Indeed, the babies went from a maternity ward to
either a foster home or institution where they were
carefully scrutinized for any possible defect. Because psychologists held the view that intelligence
could be measured through the administration of
infant tests, agencies delayed placement so as to
avoid a situation of a poor match between the
child's potential and the adopting family's expectations. Recent research evidence, however, has
cast doubt on the predictive value of such tests,
and the practice has, therefore, been virtually
abandoned. Research findings have altered the
practice from another perspective -- the potential
effects of psychic trauma, due to recurrent shifts
from one mother figure to another. Thus, the
effects of maternal separation and possible deprivation are avoided and both the child and parents can
establish a permanent bond of affectional caring
from the earliest possible age.

Contemporary placement practices have reflected
this change. The child is released from the hospital to his adoptive parents as early as is medically
permissible. Thus, the child is usually at home
with his parents two or three days after birth,
just as he would be if he had been born to them.
His parents know as little about him as any other
parent of a newborn, and they begin the parenting

4

relationship without having to accommodate to a previous parenting style.

The current practice pays considerable attention to the importance of beginning the bonding process from earliest infancy. This is particularly advantageous to the adoptive mother, since it gives her the opportunity to engage in a symbiotic experience with the infant from which each can derive emotional satisfaction. It is also advantageous to the adoptive father because he shares in the experience of parenthood. It is advantageous to the child, who is provided the opportunity for consistent parenting. It is advantageous to all of them, collectively, because it facilitates the sense of "belongingness" with each other.

CHAPTER II

LEGAL ASPECTS OF ADOPTION

Adoption is a multifaceted creation. It is a social invention, designed to give permanence to a parent-child relationship between individuals who are not so related by nature. Adoption well carried out gives the child lasting parental images with which to identify. He develops normally within a relationship in which he has received a good measure of those ingredients which sound personality growth requires. It is love and acceptance which form the basis for stability and productivity in later life. Being wanted gives a child a sense of desirability and worthiness. But being adopted is a legal contract as well, signifying a relationship binding together three individuals who have, in a sense, chosen each other.

Adoption is a beginning and an ending. It is a beginning of a lifelong relationship in which two adults voluntarily assume the rights and privileges of a parent -- rights which have to do with caring and nurturing, not to mention worrying, at appropriate times. Being a parent means being totally committed to the health and well-being of your child -- for life. At the same time, it is an ending -- the adoption signifies a termination of the parental rights of those responsible for the child's birth. Typically, the termination precedes the adoption, although frequently these two legal procedures occur virtually simultaneously. We will comment on these processes later in this chapter.

Adoption, as a practice and under legal codification, is traceable to ancient times. Biblical reference is made to its equivalent with the "adoption" of Moses by Pharoah's daughter. The

7

Babylonian Code of Hammurabi established adoption practices which were known to exist among various peoples around the world, including the ancient Romans, Greeks and Spaniards.

Attitudes towards adoption by various groups continue to exist and affect legislation (or lack of it). For example, the ancient Hebrews placed a heavy emphasis on the continuation of the family bloodline; hence, any practice that would confuse the issue as to who would be an heir was considered unthinkable. Consequently, no allowance was made for adoption, a practice which continues according to Hebrew law. In ancient Rome, the primary purpose of adoption was to assure the continuation of the male line and the family's political power through a continuation of the family name. Those states (few in number) which pattern their laws after the Spanish and French follow the Roman practice of sanctioning adoption.

These Spanish or continental law states are the exception rather than the rule. For the most part, our American laws are derived from and patterned after English law; hence, the term "Anglo-American jurisprudence." But there was no body of English law regarding adoption. In fact, there was no legal process for adoption before 1926. In England, prior to this time, people who sought to adopt could only do so by a special act of Parliament. Therefore, America had no model to follow.

In the United States, however, there was pressing need for the establishment of secure and legal family ties, as literally thousands of children were homeless and families were desirous of adopting them. The latter part of the nineteenth century and first part of the twentieth century were times of great social movement and reform, and children were the greatest beneficiaries (child

labor laws as an example). Massachusetts was one
of the first states to enact an adoption statute,
which occurred in 1851, and the statute served as
a model in other states. By 1929, every state had
passed an adoption law and, although the statutes
varied to some extent, the general legislation
suggested an emphasis on the protection of the
various principals involved -- the biological and
adoptive parents, the child and the community.

There are several legal concepts implicit in
adoption work, both of which are traceable to the
English system. The first has already been discussed in some detail and pertains to the process
by which a child unrelated by birth becomes a
family member. The second legal concept is the
right of the state to place a child with the family
with which it deems most appropriate. The state's
parental function in matters pertaining to children derives from the tradition of *parens patriae*,
which means that the state is the ultimate "parent"
of each child and is charged with the responsibility
to act on the child's behalf. Under the English
system, the King authorized his representatives
(Chancellors) to protect all infants in the realm,
but authority was limited to those situations that
threatened their present or future well-being. Today
the term *parens patriae* has been defined as the
responsibility to do what is in the "best interest
of the child," and this is the generally accepted
standard used in the courts.

These are the concepts which permit a child to
be adopted. The actual legal steps, however, involve a two-step process of termination of the birth
parents' rights and responsibilities and an acceptance of these same rights and responsibilities by
the adopters. Whether or not this is done in a
singular court proceeding or in two distinct and
separate judicial proceedings depends on the circumstances of the individual case and the way the law

9

is written in that particular state.

A birth parent may relinquish parental rights to a child in one of two ways. He or she may consent to adoption in an expressed manner, or the relinquishment of parental rights may be implicit in nature.

If a child is voluntarily relinquished to an agency or attorney for placement with adoptive parents, the birth parent consents by signing a contract, stating, in essence, "I forfeit my parental rights. I have been fully advised as to the alternatives. It is best for my child that I do this. I cannot take care of the child. No one is forcing me to do this." As in any contract, there can be no force or coercion involved in obtaining the signature. The consent cannot be purchased with cash or any other thing of value, and must be a free and voluntary act in order to constitute a valid, binding and enforceable contract. This process is called an express waiver of parental rights.

The implied waiver of parental rights is less clear-cut. For instance, if a birth parent abandons an infant, the child could be placed in a foster home awaiting adoption or placed directly into a potential adoptive home. Because of the concern about children's welfare, as expressed through the doctrine of *parens patriae*, the law does not permit a child to remain in an uncertain situation or status for an extended period of time. Something must be done about it. After a certain period of time, consent is implied in accordance with the law of that particular state, and parental rights are terminated by judicial decree. In the situation just described (implied-in-law consent), there has been either no voluntary display of parental responsibility towards the child and/or

a failure to support the child for a requisite
period of time.

      Generally, it is the birth mother who initiates
relinquishment of parental rights. If the parents
are unmarried, the birth father has historically
been given little recognition in the legal process.
The Supreme Court of the United States does, however, dictate that parental rights may not be terminated without notification of the birth father regarding the impending adoption. This decision grew
out of a precedent-setting case in 1972: Stanley
vs. Illinois. Mr. Stanley and his common law wife
had several children. Illinois had a statute which
held that the children of unwed fathers become wards
of the state in the event of the mother's death,
without any notice of such proceeding being given
to the putative father. The mother died and, accordingly, the Cook County Department of Public Welfare
in Chicago took the children and placed them in foster
homes without any notification to Mr. Stanley.
Mr. Stanley sued the State of Illinois, holding that
the statute was unconstitutional on the grounds that
it violated the Fourteenth Amendment due process and
equal protection clauses. His argument was that he
was dealt with differently than other parents, all
of whom would have been provided a hearing on their
fitness before their children are removed from their
custody. The case went to the United States Supreme
Court, which decided, in effect, that regardless of
status, the birth father was entitled to notice that
foster or adoptive placement of his children was
pending. Mr. Stanley was then granted a hearing.
It was determined, however, that placement with him
was not in the children's best interests and the
children were removed permanently from his care.
The result of this Supreme Court action, however,
had far-reaching overtones. All of the state legislatures, fearing similar cases, passed statutes requiring notification of the birth father, entitling
him to a hearing.

Therefore, even if the birth mother signs a waiver of rights, notice must be given to the birth father, and if he so desires, he may present his case in court. Should he declare a willingness and ability to care for the child, the court must balance his interests against those of the potential adoptive parents who have also expressed a desire for the responsibility of raising the child. Often the birth father is young and, for practical reasons, is simply unwilling to take on the financial and emotional obligations involved in supporting a child. Even when he expresses willingness to support the child, the court frequently decides that it is in the best interests of the child to be placed with the two-parent adoptive family, seen as more stable than the individual birth father.

The court decisions have divided the birth father's circumstances into two categories. The first situation involves what the court believes to be a casual relationship. The second situation is one in which there is greater permanency of the man-woman relationship, such as living together over a period of time. In the former situation, the birth father is entitled to only minor consideration, but in the latter situation, his claims to the child are elevated substantially.

Under present laws, all records concerning adoption proceedings and the original birth certificate are sealed and held confidential. Currently, there is a highly emotional controversy raging over the opening of sealed court records to allow the adopted child knowledge about his biological origins. The issue has understandably become a conflict of rights between the child, the birth parents and the adoptive parents.

In order to put this matter in proper perspective, one needs to recognize the implicit contract

12

at the time of placement. In the past, both the adoptive parents and the birth parents were led to believe that in deciding upon adoption of the child, they would be assured confidentiality and anonymity. When a birth mother voluntarily terminated her rights to a child, she was promised that her privacy would be respected and that she would live an unencumbered life with regards to that child. Having made what she believed was a final decision, she did not anticipate that later in life she might be confronted by the child she never knew. Adoptive parents, also promised privacy, did not anticipate that, with their identity disclosed, the birth parents might contact them concerning the child, nor did they anticipate that their child might search for, and possibly find, his birth parents. They often fear their loss of privacy and, with it, the possible loss of their child.

It is important to realize that the situation with regard to the sealed record controversy is in a state of flux. The basic assumptions underlying the confidentiality and anonymity guarantees have been challenged from both legal and psychological perspectives. At this particular time in our history, it must seem quite threatening to adoptive parents to learn that laws are being changed which may permit adoptees to seek out their birth parents. Part of the concern is related to a perception that the child does not love them (the adoptive parents), but part of the concern is related to the fear that the child will encounter an additional rejection or an otherwise disappointing experience.

There is, however, another group of people who may be equally threatened by the controversy -- the birth parents, particularly birth mothers. For many of them, giving up their babies years ago represented a closed chapter, one which they feel should not be reopened. And because of our tendency to allow young mothers (as young as 14 or 15) to keep their babies, we may be creating a situation in which pregnant adolescents in the future will abort the pregnancy to insure against the possibility of a future search.

Such a birth mother may think: "If I can't assure myself that the chapter will be closed, do my grieving and get it over with, I may as well go through an abortion. Then I know it will be a closed chapter." Or the fear of a search may result in keeping the child when she had no intention of doing so. She may think: "If the child is going to contact me anyway, why go through the trouble of giving him up?"

There can be no doubt that adoption serves multiple purposes and that competing interests are involved. Adoption must serve the interests of the adopter as well as the adoptee, but if adoption serves primarily the former rather than the latter's needs, a conflict situation seems inevitable. This is precisely the way adoption is perceived by many adoptees. They are now claiming that their "right to know" is legitimate and that the right of confidentiality expected by both sets of parents is no longer valid. There are tremendous variations with regard to motivation. It is dangerous to generalize based on a sample of a relative few. Some adoptees are seeking only information, such as medical histories. Some are caught up in curiosity about their genealogical backgrounds. Many are struggling with problems of identity and seek a reunion with their birth parents to answer such questions as, "Why was I placed for adoption? Did my birth parents love me? Why did they give me up? Who am I, really?" The range of questions starts with a mild curiosity at one end of the continuum and an obsessive need to actually locate the birth parents at the other end.

14

There are those who believe that the main cause of the controversy is the existence of an official denial to records rather than the child's desire to seek information about his or her background. Would allowing access to the records necessarily result in many taking advantage of the information they contain? Or, does the fact that the information is forbidden make it more enticing? Evidence from Scotland suggests that the latter may be the case. That country allows adoptees to secure knowledge from an adopted children's registry when they are age seventeen. Less than two percent actually make use of the registry.

Adoption was contrived as a final step, a break with the past and the beginning of a new life for all concerned -- because of the recognition of the need for stability and commitment between family members. Adoption's entire rationale grew out of the value of stable and productive family life. It is, indeed, difficult to reconcile the justifiable, but conflicting, rights of birth and adoptive parents and the child with what we know and understand about the values of family life. One of the predicates at the time of placement was that this was an irrevocable and final decision and that no birth parent entered into this contract thinking that, at some future point, she would be approached by a twenty-year-old who said, "You are the woman who gave me birth."

It is a highly controversial issue and presumably one in which there is no one right answer. Some of the suggestions for changing public policy regarding the sealed adoption records would address this issue by revealing the identity of birth parents only upon obtaining their permission. A procedure for implementing this policy will be discussed later in the book. But the controversy will, no doubt, continue until decisions about the opening

15

of sealed court records are made by the courts or
the legislatures.

CHAPTER III

THE ADOPTIVE PARENT

As we have noted, adoptive parents are similar to biological parents in many ways. After final approval of the adoption petition the child becomes the child of the adoptive parents, just as if he had been born to them. The adoptive parents assume the responsibility for care and welfare of the child as would any other parents, and the child becomes an integral part of the family. The adoptive parents relate to the child with all the love and care they would invest in their biological child.

However, it is important to be aware of the differences between adoptive and biological parenthood. Most of the differences derive from the fact that the child came to the family by a different route. Consequently, the societal view regarding parenthood comes into play as a distinct difference. The societal presumption is that the best parents for any given child are his biological parents. For biological parents, therefore, society must prove that they are incapable (or unwilling) of being good parents. For adoptive parents, since they fall outside this general rule in that they did not give birth to the child, proof must be given that they are capable of being good parents.

Deriving from this overall distinction, there are a number of differences. First, biological parents require no intermediary in becoming parents; yet, adoptive parents require either a social agency or an attorney and/or physician to intercede in their behalf. Biological parents need not prove their ability and readiness to assume a parental role, as adoptive parents must. Biological parents know from the outset that the child is unconditionally theirs.* Adoptive parents, on the other hand, are first faced with uncertainty about whether they will receive a

17

child. Even after they do get a child, they face an uneasy tentativeness about the permanency of the arrangement. Despite the fact that the probability is small that the child will be removed during the supervisory period by the agency or the court, fear and apprehension haunt many adoptive parents until the adoption is actually approved in court.

There are other differences as well. Biological parenthood is presumed to become a reality within a predictable period of time, giving the family an opportunity to prepare emotionally for the arrival of the child, while prospective adoptive parents are never completely certain whether and when to expect their child. It is a nerve-wrenching experience to prepare psychologically for an event which may, in reality, never come to pass. When the couple finally does get word of the birth of the child who is to be theirs, there is often such a flurry of activity in making the necessary arrangements that it may be some time before they feel the joy of receiving the child.

Adoptive parents have unique psychological hurdles to clear before they can come to terms with the realness of their parenthood. The uniqueness of their situation leads to certain feelings which are virtually inevitable. The sense of entitlement of parents to child, of child to parents, and siblings to each other is a task unique to adoption. This sense of entitlement refers to the feeling that the child really belongs to them. It is a sense of

*There are exceptions to the unconditionality. Parents are not allowed to abuse their children, as already noted in the discussion regarding parens patriae. But assuming that their children are receiving a modicum of appropriate care, the statement is true.

belonging to each other, parents to child and child to parents that is the desired objective.

This overall task is best accomplished through the achievement of certain sub-tasks. The first is to recognize and accept the differences between the two different forms of parenthood. Adoption experts agree that acknowledgment of differences, rather than their denial, will result in more relaxed communication between parents and child, and hence, a better adjustment to the adoptive situation (Kirk, 1964). A second sub-task is to recognize and deal with feelings attendant to infertility. Adults whose sense of personal competency is not contingent upon biological reproduction can do this without evoking feelings of inadequacy. The third sub-task is to handle the myriad questions and comments about the child's adoptive status, comments which reflect a societal view that suggests a superiority of biological over adoptive parenthood.

Who is, after all, the "real" parent? Is the parent the person who gave birth to the child or the person who assumes the role of guiding and caring for the child? In the Judeo-Christian tradition, the parent is identified as the one who fulfills the caring, nurturing role. One example is found in the Talmud, the moral and legal text of rabbinic Judaism, which identifies the father, not the one who gave birth, as the one who raises the child. One adoptee stated the distinction in this manner: "Your parents are not the ones who gave you your genes -- your parents are the ones who gave you your love." In this view, there are not two sets of parents -- differentiation is made between the parents and the individuals who begot the child (Krugman, 1964).

Entitlement is a very complex phenomenon and there is some evidence to suggest that it is not a question of whether or not one feels entitled, but to what degree the sense of entitlement has been developed. This partial sense of entitlement, then, may manifest itself in certain areas. It may manifest itself in problems of discipline, in allowing the child a measure of independence from them, or in telling him about the adoption. It may manifest itself in a feeling of guilt about the fact that he can never encounter his genetic past. Such adoptive parents are vulnerable because the uneasy feeling that the child is not really theirs robs them of the authority of "real parents." In a study of adoptive mothers, clinicians discovered that most of the mothers felt that they somehow did not have a right to the child (Walsh and Lewis, 1969). Another problem related to entitlement is contained in our regulatory laws and practices, which require a protracted waiting period before becoming the child's legal parents. A study by Gochros indicated that the waiting period proved troublesome to most adoptive parents (1962). Reactions to the visitations varied, but many parents perceived the social worker to be a benevolent probation officer. This muted the sense of "belongingness."

On the other hand, it should not be surprising that parents reacted to the visitations in this particular way. Ordinarily, parents do not have social workers coming to the home to evaluate the quality of care given to the children. It is a rather unnatural phenomenon. Adoptive parents are already struggling with their feelings around making the children their own and, therefore, supervisory visits might well be viewed with some degree of displeasure. It is a reminder of the fact that the children are not yet theirs.

Adoptive parents must also recognize the effect that their feelings concerning infertility may have on family life. Couples generally come to adoption out of necessity. The inability to produce a child is, in most cases, the determining factor in the desire to adopt. Many couples consider questions regarding their personal reactions toward infertility an unwarranted invasion of privacy unrelated to their ability to be good parents. The fact is that unresolved feelings of disappointment, anger or guilt concerning infertility can have a powerful effect on family life. Infertility may be perceived as a deprivation or even as a loss. Failure to come to grips with such feelings may result in a generally unhealthy atmosphere for the adopted child and the family as a whole. Elizabeth Lawder's research, in which she examined the relationship between adoptive outcome and attitudes toward infertility, suggests that the ability of the father and mother to accept infertility does have a bearing on the acceptance of the adopted child and, hence, on the child's later functioning. She states:

> The adoptive mother's ability to discuss infertility prior to placement was significantly related to outcome. Although the father's ability to discuss infertility showed a relationship to parental functioning, the degree of relationship was consistently smaller than that from the mother . . . the implication from practice is that infertility is a sensitive area . . . some couples come to an (adoption) agency after they have truly accepted their feelings . . . the association between the mother's ability to discuss infertility and parental communication of the fact of adoption to the child suggest that the better the parents understand these feelings, the better they are able to cope with the related problem of telling the child of his adoption (p. 167).

Again, let us stress it is not the fact of infertility that is the crucial variable, but the resulting feelings about having missed the opportunity to take an active part in the biological procreative process.

Actually, our knowledge of how couples react to the news of childlessness is rather sparse and has come from limited data. However, in general, the reaction can be likened to a reaction to any severe crisis. It can be a severe blow. For many, the revelation is so fraught with painful feelings of disappointment and inferiority that they must deny the reality. Others react with a sense of helplessness at losing control over their life's plans. In time, the denial is replaced by anger, as the couple asks, "Why us?" Couples may question which partner is "at fault" and begin to doubt the security of their marriage. The experience leads the individual to feel a sense of failure. It is important to recognize that these feelings do not relate to the reality, but the feelings are there, nonetheless. One is apt to hear one spouse saying to the other, "If you had married someone else, you would have a child by now." The feeling that one has betrayed the bloodline is difficult to counteract.

In part, this reaction is linked to our folklore, and in our experience it is more likely to involve the woman. One frequently heard remark is, "You're not a woman until you have had a baby." In addition, in our culture at least, women are considered to be the adult family member most responsible for the maintenance of family ties. While men are considered most responsible for maintaining the family outside the home through their work or professions, women are ordinarily viewed as the carriers of the responsibility for maintaining family ties within the home. Another reaction, culturally derived, is the feeling that one does not deserve to enjoy sex since a baby is not being produced. Again, this derives from sexual

22

mythology which states that the purpose of sex is to procreate. This situation is changing, of course, but there is always a time lag between changing ideologies and our ways of instituting them.

There are a number of phases characteristic of this process, once the initial shock or sense of disbelief wears off. Couples typically go through these phases, even though they vary in length and tend to overlap with each other (Mazor, 1979). During the first phase, the couple wonders why the infertility has happened to them or what they might have done to warrant being singled out. In attempting to deal with this reaction, couples go through a number of medical procedures and tests, some of which are physically painful and some of which are psychologically demeaning. Others go through a bargaining phase, offering to suffer in return for a baby. Perhaps the most poignant example of bargaining is contained in the biblical account of Hannah, who promised to give her son (if God granted her wish) to the Lord all the days of the child's life (1 Samuel 1:11). In the second phase, grief and mourning are experienced with considerable intensity. It is during this phase that denial gives way to anger. It is also during this phase that couples come to terms with their fantasied loss and many, in fact, report that the shared mourning experience has brought them closer together than ever before. The third stage is characterized by coming to terms with the nature of the situation with which they are faced. Of utmost importance is the couple's ability and willingness to share feelings with each other and to recognize that they are natural and normal.

For the couple able to acknowledge such feelings, there follows a desire to handle them through discussion with each other or professional counseling. Feelings of inferiority can be alleviated by restoring confidence in parental capacity, by a hope that one

can continue to satisfy the partner emotionally and
by an intellectual recognition that sexual capability
and reproductive productivity are not synonymous.
There may be renewed desire for a child, and the
compensatory wish to give of oneself to a child becomes stronger. Finally, couples who cannot procreate realize that they can find great satisfaction
in contributing to a child's growth and development.
It is not procreation which makes the parent, but
the sense that one is contributing meaningfully to
the life of another human being. Through this recognition, parents can find enormous satisfaction and
fulfillment.

How does a couple know when they have resolved
their feelings about infertility? Generally, an
ability to discuss adoption openly is usually an
indication of a relatively healthy resolution. There
are several clues that are suggestive, however, of
failure to resolve these feelings, including pro-
longed denial of the existence of feelings of disappointment, obsessive fears that a child will not
measure up to family standards, anxiety about discussing adoption, discussing the child's adoption
under virtually any circumstances, fantasies about
one's imagined biological child, unabating resentment
toward visits by the agency social worker or inappropriate sharing of the fact of adoption with family,
friends or acquaintances.

At any time during the child's life, but preferably early, couples should feel free to make use of
professional services. The need to make use of such
services should not be interpreted as a perceived
defect in one's psychological armor. There are two
ways this can be done. Individual counseling by one
trained in helping couples deal with the special
psychological tasks can lead to a greater sense of
entitlement. Groups on adoptive parenting can also
be helpful. Groups are valuable ways of satisfying

24

a natural desire of people for group belonging and peer acceptance. Group discussions provide a means by which parents can talk about and reveal the myriad ways in which each family deals with both adoptive and growth problems. Besides revealing problems, the group discussions demonstrate how gratifying their parenting experiences have been and how their lives have changed. It is necessary to know that there are others who also struggle with the special problems of adoptive parenthood, and it is comforting to see that these struggles do not make them poor parents or any less the parents of their children.

Once adoptive parents make the psychological adjustments to their unique situation, they still must confront the task of dealing with the societal attitude towards the institution of adoption. Some of the difficulties in rearing adopted children stem from community or societal attitudes which grant less than unconditional acceptance to parenthood via adoption. This societal ambivalence is reflected in our patterns of speech and our mores. Consider one of our best known axioms: "Blood is thicker than water." Such views lead to a certain defensiveness in adoptive parents, who are expected to respond undefensively to remarks from relatives as, "It's too late to give him back now." People who make such tactless remarks obviously do not realize the prejudice these remarks contain nor their potential for hurting.

Consider also the terms we use in describing birth parents: "natural," "real," "own." This may imply that adoptive parents are somehow unnatural or unreal or that parenthood by adoption is an inferior form of parenthood. Yet, these terms continue to be used, not only by lay persons, but also by professionals in the field, seemingly unaware of the biological chauvinism they are fostering.

Even some apparently positive attitudes contain seeds of doubt about the legitimacy of adoption. Undue congratulations containing subtle messages are heaped on the couple. Remarks like "How lucky for the child to have parents like you!" are not infrequently made. Many remarks of this nature reflect the rescue fantasy by implying that the child, perhaps the product of a union between "inadequate" people, is rescued from a life of blight and neglect. Such remarks would rarely, if ever, be made to parents following the birth of their child. In fact, one would more likely say to new (biological) parents, "How lucky you are to have such a beautiful child!"

In an interesting study of community attitudes toward adoption, Kirk found that nine out of ten couples heard such remarks as "Isn't it wonderful of you to have taken in this child!" and "This child looks so much like you that he (she) could be your own!" Four of five were asked, "Tell me, what do you know about the child's background?" One out of two parents was told: "He is a darling baby, and after all, you never know for sure how even your own will turn out." One out of three heard: "How lucky you didn't have to go through the trouble of pregnancy like I did." And, one out of five heard: "How well you care for the child, just like a real mother!"

On the other hand, adoption is often viewed in positive terms. People who adopt children are congratulated by relatives, friends and other well-wishers. Baby gifts are sent and the entire occasion is recognized publicly. Some parents even send announcements, modified to reflect the unique way the child came into the family. One such announcement came in the form of a legal document.*

*The writers are indebted to Melvin Daniel for the development of this "petition," the names of which are fictionalized.

26

STATE OF BLISS)   SS: IN THE FAIRYLAND FEDERAL COURT
COUNTY OF NOD)   1980 SPRING TERM

IN RE THE MATTER OF THE BIRTH)   CAUSE NO. B80-1
OF JEAN LYNN JONES, INFANT   )

PETITION FOR ORDER FOR NOTICE TO INTERESTED PARTIES

    Comes now John R. Jones and Marilyn A. Jones, husband and wife, Petitioners herein, and for their Petition say as follows:

    1. That on January 5, 1980, at 4:30 A.M., a little girl was born.
    2. That the said little girl weighed seven (7) pounds and thirteen (13) ounces at birth.
    3. That the said little girl was twenty-one (21) inches long at birth.
    4. That on January 6, 1980, the Cook Superior Court, Probate Division, entered an Order placing the temporary custody of said child with your Petitioners herein, namely, John R. Jones and Marilyn A. Jones, for the purpose of adoption of said infant.
    5. That the said little girl is to be named Jean Lynn Jones.
    6. That the said little girl, namely, Jean Lynn Jones, is a delight to her parents, John R. Jones and Marilyn A. Jones, your Petitioners herein, and her sister, Sally Jones.
    7. That although said child is not flesh of our flesh nor bone of our bone, nevertheless, she is still miraculously our own, and that no one should forget for one minute that she didn't grow under our heart -- but in it.

    WHEREFORE, your Petitioners pray that the Court ORDER that all interested parties be duly notified of the above-described event.

Respectfully submitted,

_____
John R. Jones, Petitioner

_____
Marilyn A. Jones, Petitioner

O R D E R

SO ORDERED this 10th day of January, 1980.

_____
Justine Equity, JUDGE,
Fairyland Federal Court

The child is viewed in these cases as an integral part
of his new family.

The real joys of adoptive parenting come not
from these congratulatory remarks, but from the sense
of fulfillment in watching one's child grow and contributing to his development. These, of course, are
simply the joys of parenthood, joys which adoptive
parents can experience as fully as other parents, provided they have resolved the conflicts previously
identified and developed a sense of entitlement to
their child.

CHAPTER IV

THE TELLING

Undoubtedly, the most unique aspect of adoption is "the telling" -- to relatives, friends, neighbors and, most importantly, to the child himself. For a host of reasons, the telling is the most difficult and problematic aspect of adoption. Adopters may feel that it may produce problems for both child and parent, or it may resurrect problems once thought to be resolved.

First, the telling produces for the child another and perhaps competitive set of parents. The very act of telling brings birth parents into the family system and can thereby jeopardize the exclusiveness of the parent-child relationship. Second, if the adoptive parents are still struggling to develop feelings of entitlement, anxious feelings may suddenly surface. This complicates the telling, as the child will respond more to the anxiety of the parents than to the content they wish to convey. Third, the parents are faced with the need to explain why they needed to resort to adoption. If they have not previously resolved the issue of infertility, the telling may stir up anxious feelings about sexual adequacy.

So, how do you tell a child he is adopted? Most books recommend that parents explain adoption in a matter-of-fact manner and convey their acceptance of the child and his background through their willingness to discuss the adoption.

This advice is all well and good. Unfortunately, the research is unclear about how to accomplish this objective. Certain principles, however, may suggest a clue and, of course, if the parents have worked through their feelings about whose child this really

29

is, the "homework," in a sense, has been done.

The basic principle underlying the telling is this: The ease with which the child fully accepts his adoptedness is directly related to the degree of success the adoptive parents have achieved in accepting their own status of adoptive parents. There are several clues which indicate the degree of acceptance. If they do not avoid this sensitive issue or feel the need to reveal it with every conceivable opportunity, but can discuss it openly, without fear, guilt or embarrassment, the indications are that acceptance has taken place. If, on the other hand, they are struggling with fantasies of how their own biological children might have looked and behaved or reacting emotionally or defensively to the news of a friend's pregnancy or birth of a friend's child, this indicates that underlying attitudes need to be more fully explored. Under such circumstances, discussions about adoption may take place at inappropriate times and convey to the child a sense that something is wrong. Either too much talking about adoption or not talking about it at all indicates that there are problems in acceptance. Parents should also realize that children respond more readily to feelings and nuances than they do to what is being said.

A case example will dramatize this point.

A fertility specialist referred a couple to an adoption agency the same day they learned that pregnancy was considerably in doubt. The couple, but the woman in particular, recalled how distraught they were when it came time to pick up the baby, a four-month-old infant son. (Obviously, the grieving was most incomplete.) Years later, she told the clinical social worker how she felt she and

30

her husband had "stolen" the child.
There was a good deal of disappointment
in that the child did not develop
according to expectations. When she
explained adoption to the child, she
told him how much he was wanted, but
the message that got through to the boy
was how his birth parents had not
wanted him and stressed, inadvertently,
how his adoptive parents had rescued
him. The boy never asked about adoption again.

In situations where unresolved feelings create
anxiety when the subject of adoption is broached,
such anxiety can often be a clue suggestive of
poor resolution. Or, when adoption is discussed
repeatedly, to the point of "overkill," the warning
signal is that something has gone awry in the
telling of the child's adoption. The effect of
this on the child may be to threaten his identification with, and integration into, the adoptive
family. These polar positions of too little or
too much telling reflect an inability to deal with
adoption.

Actually, the whole idea of telling has come
under scrutiny in recent years. Some critics
question its wisdom on the grounds that the knowledge of different birth origins is too painful
for a child and that he is better off spared such
information. These critics argue that the child
need not deal with such an emotionally charged
issue as the reality of two sets of parents nor
bear the impact of original rejection. Other
critics suggest that while the adoptee has the
right to know about the fact of his birth, the
telling should be delayed until he is of school
age and has already passed through the most forma-
tive years of his life. The basis of such views

31

comes from clinical impressions of a sample made up of emotionally troubled children who have, coincidentally, been adopted.

However plausible these arguments, the fact is that there are grave risks associated with both the "no telling" and "delayed telling" approaches. First, such approaches falsify a relationship which is supposed to be based on openness and honesty. Honesty is a crucial element in a healty parent-child relationship. Without honesty, there can be no relationship. Adopted children who do not learn of their adoption until late adolescence or early adulthood invariably experience feelings of betrayal and profound hurt. Ultimately, this child may come to believe that if something as funda-mental and basic as a relationship between parent and child is based on a lie, then all else is a lie as well. Second, the very act of withholding the information suggests to the child that there is something wrong with adoption. The child may well think, "If my own parents can't talk about my adoption, there must be something wrong with it." By extension, he may also decide, "There must be something wrong with me." Third, there is always the possibility that, since adoption is invariably a matter of public knowledge to relatives and friends, the child will hear of it first from another source. Fourth, the child is entitled to know the truth about his origins. The question, therefore, involves ethi-cal considerations.

When the child asks, "Where did I come from?", it is important to answer his question openly and without hesitation. Many adoptive parents dread this occasion, particularly if they have not suffi-ciently worked through their own feelings about being adoptive parents. But the telling can be a most gratifying experience, one which adds to, rather than detracts from, a feeling of belonging and

32

identity. Instead of perceiving the occasion as
a threat to the parent-child relationship, parents
should view it as a challenge and as a way of
solidifying a positive bond. Research findings
confirm this view: The more open the subject of
adoption, the better the child's adjustment to it.

When, then, should a child be told of his
adoption? There is no universally correct answer.
Timing depends on the readiness of the individual
child. Children differ in their maturational and
intellectual development, and some children are
ready sooner than others. Generally, by the age of
three to four, a child should have heard the word
"adoption" and should have some idea of how he
came to live with his parents. We suggest drawing
a picture of the home, the hospital and the agency
or attorney's office, so that the child can visual-
ize the interrelated aspects of his "coming home".
For the young child, mere words are not enough.
The pictorial presentation may give him a clearer
understanding of how he and his parents came together (see Figure 1).

Figure 1.

When the child is a little older, perhaps four or five, he may ask questions again. Although there is no one right formula for words to use in the telling, the following dialogue suggests some of the more typical questions posed by children, along with possible answers.

Child: Mommy, where did I come from?

Mother: Why do you ask, honey?

Child: Johnny says he came from his mommy's tummy. Did I come from your tummy?

Mother: No, you didn't.

Child: Well, where did I come from, then?

Mother: Good question. Do you remember us using the word "adoption"?

Child: Yes.

Mother: What do you remember it means?

Child: You said it means you wanted me because you and Daddy couldn't have a baby of your own.

Mother: Right, which also means that you came out of another woman's tummy. She was not able to care for you, so she asked that another family be picked out to love you and give you the care she was unable to give you but wanted you to have.

Child: You mean that you're not my real mommy?

Mother: Is that how you feel, that I'm not your real mommy?

35

Child: No, I think you are -- but this is
        all so confusing.

Mother: I know it's hard to understand. It's
        different, but now that you have a
        better idea about what adoption is
        all about, I want you to know it is
        the only difference, because we're
        glad we have you and you are one of
        us. You are my child just the same
        as Johnny is his mother's child, and
        I love you and want you just the same
        as if you had come from my own tummy.

Child: Okay. Well, I'll see you, Mommy. I
        want to go out to the backyard and
        play on the swings with the other kids.

There are several important aspects in this conversation worthy of note. First, the mother does not
answer the child's question until she understands
exactly what he has on his mind.* Second, she helps
him make connections between what was told on previous occasions and what she is about to disclose.
Third, she feels reasonably comfortable in revealing
his origins to him, and he can accept the reality,
because she accepts it. Finally, the child is allowed
to express his feelings about what he has been told
and about what adoption means to him. The child responds in kind to the mother's warmth and openness in

---

*Some parents remember the joke about the child who
came home and asked where he came from; whereupon, the
parent went into a long, detailed explanation of where
children come from, including all the sexuality and reproductive organs, and so on. At the end of the explanation, the child scratched his head and said, "Well, my
friend down the street said he came from Philadelphia,
and I was wondering where I came from."

discussing a matter of great importance to him. The "sugarcoating" that frequently goes along with the telling, such as "we chose you" and "you are the chosen child" is omitted.

Imagine the impact on the child whose parent followed the path of not telling, or who suggested that the child was too young. The child's natural curiosity would have been thwarted and an invitation to the world of fantasy would have been expedited. He may well have emerged from that very important encounter feeling that there was something wrong with his question or, worse, that there was something wrong with him. Instead, the mother in our dialogue revealed the truth to the child while reassuring him of her love for him and of his place in the family.

It has proved positive in our experience to refer to the birth mother as "the woman who gave birth" rather than the "mother." Particularly for children under the age of five, the idea of two mothers may be confusing. Because the child at this stage is ill-equipped to handle such confusion, we suggest that the terms "mother" and "father" be reserved for those who have accepted the parenting and nurturing role.

A final caution regarding the telling, as indicated earlier: It can be overdone. While avoidance of the subject matter may carry confusing and unhealthy messages to the child, overemphasis is also undesirable. The child wants to know about the adoption, but he does not want the fact reiterated at every opportunity. In McWhinnie's Studies of Adult Adoptees, she noted:

> None of these adopted children wanted
> their adoptive status shrouded in complete
> secrecy . . . Equally, they did not want
> constant reference to it. They wanted

something in between, where their adopted
status was acknowledged without embarrassment and then overtly forgotten so that
they were treated exactly as if they were
biological sons and daughters of the
adopted parents . . . Thus, they were em-
phatic that they did not want to be introduced as an "adopted son" or an "adopted
daughter" . . . They wanted to feel they
belonged in the family and were completely
accepted there as a son or a daughter
(p. 249).

It is important to recognize that children's
reactions vary and that not all children accept
the "moment of truth" as well as the child in our
dialogue. These reactions, and their underlying
meanings, will be dealt with in the following
chapter.

CHAPTER V

THE ADOPTED CHILD

Adopted parents, like all parents, are concerned about their child's psychological development. The questions seem to center around what type of person their son or daughter will turn out to be. Perhaps the questions are more pressing for adoptive parents than for biological parents, but this may be an assumption. At any rate, it has been our experience that adoptive parents do manifest this concern, and it is, therefore, appropriate to devote some time to a contemporary understanding of the psychological development of the adopted child.

Briefly stated, we can say that while it is true that the adopted child needs to work through some feelings not faced by the nonadopted child, there is no reason to conclude that the adopted child is at greater risk in the development of a normal and stable personality. Our clinical experience and research findings that center on the relationship between adoptive status and outcome conclude that healthy personality development is based on the quality of one's family life, not on whether or not a child was adopted. Nevertheless, the adopted child and his family do face some feelings unique to the adoptive situation.

Once a child understands the meaning of adoption, he must face the idea that his birth parents decided not to rear him. This can be devastating to a child who has not been received with unqualified love and acceptance by his adoptive parents. How well a child deals with the idea of his being adopted varies according to the quality of the parent-child relationship. But the fantasy life of the adoptee must be taken into account as well.

Every child, biological or adopted, has recourse
to a particular fantasy when he has suffered hurt
upon being reprimanded by his parents. This fantasy,
known in the literature as the "family romance,"
takes root in the idea that the parents with whom
he lives are not his "real parents." His "real parents,"
according to the fantasy, were rich and famous or of
noble blood and were somehow separated from the child.
They may be "super parents" -- never scolding and for-
ever gift-giving. The child believes he will achieve
the status in life to which he, of noble ancestry, is
entitled. The child resorts to this fantasy whenever
he feels frustrated and disappointed by his parents.
The fantasy generally is of brief duration and is
abandoned once the child realizes that he can both love
and hate the same person.

It is important to remember that all children
have these fantasies. Children who live within the
security of their biological families can afford the
luxury of indulging in the fantasy as a game. For
them, it bears no relationship to reality and, therefore, need not be taken too seriously. For the adopted
child, however, there may be some reality in the fantasy.
He may fantasize about the people who brought him into
the world, wonder where they are and wonder what they
are like as people. The recognition that he was once
given up or rejected may be compounded by a sense of
dual identification or "genealogical bewilderment." The
sense of belonging can be considerably more problematic
for the adopted child. Parents who struggle continuously
with their right to the child may communicate a message
that contributes to the child's feeling that he perhaps
does not belong to this particular family. That is why
it is so important for parents to come to terms with
their own feelings about who is the real parent.

For parents who have resolved their own feelings
about biological inadequacy, who can discuss adoption
calmly, who love and accept their children regardless

40

of how they came to be part of the family, the existence of such fantasies in their adopted children
is of little consequence. If, however, parents view
the child, even unconsciously, as a symbol of their
biological inadequacy, if the child is used by one
or both parents to satisfy their own emotional needs
or as a pawn in a marital power struggle, if the
parent or parents find themselves fleeing from any
discussion of adoption, or if a distrustful or sus-
picious relationship exists between the child and
either parent, then the situation is ripe for faulty
resolution of the dilemma which results in a split
parental identification.

Considerably more important than the family
romance fantasy, from the standpoint of the child's
healthy emotional development, is his ability to
attain complete identification with his family. The
success or failure of this identification, and extent
of identification, is dependent on certain variables:
The marital relationship, its openness and authenticity,
the degree of communication and intimacy between family
members, the mutuality of support of members for one
another and how the family functions as a unit. The
reason why social workers look at these areas in the
home study is out of a recognition that while parenthood brings rewards and enrichment of experiences, it
also brings demands and responsibilities which may be
overwhelming in an already existing precarious marriage.

The problem of the child's identifying with adoptive parents is that it cannot be done or, at best, is
done with some difficulty, if the child hears dis-
paraging or critical remarks about his birth parents.
Since part of his identity is tied up with his genetic
background, such critical remarks will only serve the
purpose of fostering an identification with them. The
research evidence seems to suggest that the process
of identification is one of the most crucial in the
development of the growing child (Jolowicz, 1969). It

certainly explains why a given child will identify
with adults he has never seen, but fantasized about,
through the accounts given him by his adoptive parents.
It might be well, at this point, to examine the nature
of the process of identification as a vital ingredient
in personality development.

A child's personality takes shape as the child
learns and accepts the standards and values of his
own parents. He learns what behavior is acceptable
and what is not, by virtue of the example set for him
within the context of a meaningful, growth-producing
relationship. The adoptive parent who says, "You're
mine despite the fact that someone else gave you birth,"
tells the child that his "real" family is his adoptive
family. If all such messages are this direct and
honest, development may take place unimpeded. On the
other hand, if parents express their disappointment
in the child's behavior and relate to it by drawing
attention to the child's heredity, he receives an un-
intended message that disavows his place in the family.

There are a number of measures parents can take
to solidify the child's identity. Memorabilia in one
form or another should be made available to him/her.
Photographs taken on the day he came to the family
should be placed in his growth book. Every child
should have such a book, whether adopted or not. It
becomes a part of him. There are, however, children's
growth books specifically for adopted children. We do
not recommend such books, because we believe this draws
an undue amount of attention to the fact of adoption.

Another measure to be taken by the parents to
solidify the child's identity is through the pictorial
presentation of the family tree. Children's growth
books usually contain a tree in one form or another,
and children are frequently asked to draw a family
tree as part of a school assignment. It is essential
that the child complete this assignment with the names

42

of his parents and relatives of his adoptive family. Parents who suggest completing the family tree, using the information of genetic forebears, are inadvertently fostering an identification with his birth family. This leads to tremendous confusion and doubts over his real identity.

The child knows there are two individuals someplace who are part of him and whose genetic characteristics affect his growth and physical development. He does not need constant reminding. That is why we recommend against celebrating the adoption anniversary as a day of special note. We recognize that such a celebration may be received as a source of pride. However, even when well-handled, it focuses too much attention on the adoption. On the other hand, parents must recognize that being adopted is different, and it is a difference that must be accepted as a fact of life, both for the adopters as well as the adoptee.

The most grievous error parents can make is to assume their child does not have feelings about being adopted. The question, "Why was I adopted?", contains within it other implied questions, perhaps the most basic of which are, "Why was I given up?", "Was I so unacceptable, so unlovable, that I had to be given away as if I were a piece of merchandise?", "Was I so undesirable that a decision was made for me to deprive me of my birthright?" Such questions are painful, and there is increasing evidence that children between the ages of six and adolescence continually contend with such questions. The realization that one was once given up, or rejected, can be quite a blow to the growing child's developing sense of self-worth.

Our guiding principle is that it is not only beneficial, but necessary to allow the child to express these feelings of hurt and rejection. Children who are allowed to express their hurt are, in the long run, emotionally healthier than children who are unable or unwilling to express their feelings. Once

these feelings are expressed, the parent can univer-
salize the emotion by suggesting that virtually all
adopted children experience what the child is ex-
periencing and that it is normal to have and to express such feelings. It is then, and only then,
appropriate for the parent to reassure the child
that he is loved and wanted by them and that he is
as valued as if born to them. A comment by the
mother, such as, "I would have been very proud to
have had you grow in my body," is appropriate because it is true and because it tends to dilute the
child's fantasy of his own undesirability.

Adoptive parents should also recognize, in
this connection, that all children, adopted or not,
get angry at their parents from time to time and
contend with mixed feelings. This has nothing really
to do with adoption, but, because the parents are in
an adoptive situation, there may be a tendency to
relate the child's behavior to it. Adoptive parents
must take caution to be aware of the tendency to
perceive all experiences with their children through
the adoptive lens. Parents should relate to the
feelings the children have without interpreting
those feelings as an indictment of the parents.

Dealing specifically with a child's perceived
rejection varies with the individuals involved.
Honesty is absolutely essential. Parents should
not expect to have a single "right" answer. What
is said is less important than the feelings of
acceptance behind the words. It is important not
to be too critical of the birth mother, as this may
invite the child to defend her and, hence, to identify too strongly with her. Conversely, it is inad-
visable to lavish her with such praise that the child
sees her as victimized and distraught over the sacri-
ficial decision that was made.

Middle ground is probably best. The following
is an appropriate explanation: "We don't know a

great deal about the woman who gave birth to you, but we do know that she found herself in a diffi- cult position and wanted to make the right decision for you. She wanted you to have a better life than she could provide for you, and she found that through adoption you could be given a good home with a mother and father who would love you and care for you as she felt you should be cared for. Having made her decision probably before you were born, she was then in a better position to work out her own situation; i.e., go back to school, work, or whatever. She made this decision knowing it was final." By emphasizing that the woman probably made her decision prior to the child's birth, the child is less likely to feel that she took a look at him and decided he was unlovable.

In any explanation, the parent must take care not to stress that the birth mother made her decision out of love. There is really no way of knowing whether love entered the picture. But what we do know is that it was a perceived inability to provide the right kind of home. If adoption is explained primarily in terms of love, there may always be the fear that the adoptive parent may do likewise, since the adoptive parent professes to love the child. The important underlying principle is that the adop- tive parent must help the child achieve a positive self-image, a feeling that he is good and lovable.

This is not to suggest, however, that because the child was once rejected the parent should protect him from any measure of criticism or correction. There is no reason for the parent to feel he or she must make up for the original hurt. We suggest that the parents recognize the hurt and confusion and relate to the child just as if he had been born to them, without any special compensatory efforts. To the extent that the parents become good role models for the child and to the extent that he has been accepted and integrated into the fabric of the family, the child's identification will be with the adoptive parent and not with his birth parents. The message to the child that he is a good person, loved and valued for himself and that he will turn out to be a responsible adult is the best guarantee that such will, in fact, come to pass.

An actual interview with a young adult adoptee dramatizes the points made in the foregoing discussion:

Q: When do you recall hearing the word "adoption" for the first time, and what did that mean to you?

A: I remember it when I was five, and I remember it meaning that there was someone who loved me, but for some reason couldn't keep me and gave me up for adoption. My parents came along wanting a child and I just happened to be there at the right moment and they chose me.

Q: They told you that you were chosen? Did they use that word?

A: Yes. They always brought out that I was chosen and that I was very much loved, because if I wasn't loved, they wouldn't have chosen me.

Q: Did you ever get the fantasy that they went to the agency and picked you out?

A: No.

Q: Was it ever presented that way -- that you were a chosen child and they came and got you among a number of other kids? Did that fantasy ever hit you?

46

A: No, because they told me it was an agency and it was a place where babies who, for one reason or another, cannot be kept by their parents and are placed there until they can find a home for them.

Q: Do you think sometimes parents, adoptive parents, go through too much of the gushiness that their children were chosen, that they were special, that they were picked, and this sort of thing?

A: I think some people overdo it. Some people need to reassure themselves by reassuring the child and letting him know that he was chosen. In our family, it only came up when they were explaining the adoption process, but other than that, it was just something that was known and accepted. It was nothing that was brought up constantly. The only thing that was ever really brought up was the fact that I was loved very much. But, you know, I have a very good friend who was adopted, and right after she was adopted her mother became pregnant, and my friend has always been like the unwanted stepsister, you know, like Cinderella of the family. Her parents always say, "We chose you, we wouldn't have you here if we didn't want you here," but she has never had that feeling.

Q: She has never had the feeling that she was wanted?

A: Right. I mean, she feels like their biological children are more important to them.

Q: She feels that she is somehow different from the other siblings?

47

A: Yes.

Q: In other words, she never felt the same kind of acceptance she believes her siblings get?

A: Right.

Q: Do you think parents can make the mistake of going too far to try to get the child to accept adoption -- even to the point of bringing up the subject at inappropriate times, such as introducing the child as their adopted son or daughter?

A: I don't think that so much because I was never introduced as my parents' adopted daughter, but if the comment came up, my parents readily said, "Yes, she's adopted." Once my mother ran into an acquaintance in the bank who said, "Oh, your daughter looks so much like you, she's so cute." And my mom said, "Well, thank you, she's adopted." And nobody will believe that when they see my mother and me. That was done in a kind of light and joking manner, and I was about seven or eight at the time, and I was still incorporating the fact of being adopted into my personality; I was still working with it, and I was understanding more and more of the concepts behind it, and to hear that reinforced the value that, yes, I am adopted. That is nothing to be ashamed of. I am really proud of the fact that my parents do love me, they care for me, they wanted me, and I think that shows an abundance of acceptance on my mother's part, too, that she could have told people. She wasn't ashamed of the fact that my sister and I were both adopted and that she couldn't

48

have children. That was something that I
have always appreciated. Her pride made
me feel proud.

Q: What effect do you think it has on adopted
children if the parents don't want to talk
about adoption to them?

A: I think it lowers their self-esteem quite
a bit, because if parents won't talk to
them about it, I think they are troubled
by it. I think, if anything, it would
give the child a negative attitude toward
adoption.

Q: Make them feel as if there is something
wrong with it?

A: Right, it would make them feel that it is
an evil power of sorts.

Q: What do some of the adages we have grown
up with do to you, such as "blood is
thicker than water" or "you're a chip off
the old block"?

A: I've never really thought about them, because I know that I couldn't be closer to
anybody than I am with my parents. I've
got plenty of friends who are biological
children that aren't as close to their
parents as I am to mine, so I just consider
these adages sayings and that's about as
far as it goes.

Q: As you talk, I get the distinct feeling
that when you think about your parents, you
think about your adoptive parents. There
isn't that other fantasy person who gave
you birth?

A: No.

Q: Is this something that you can talk about a little bit?

A: I know that there is someone else out in this world who brought me into this world, but to me that person is an abstract being. I know she exists, but because I have no relationship with her, she means absolutely nothing to me.

Q: As you fantasize about your birth mother, I think you made the comment that she was a nonentity, she had no form, really. She was out there, but really. very unreal to you. Is that what you're saying?

A: Yes, I know she exists in reality, but that is a part of reality that I have never experienced, so it is not a part of me. I do wonder sometimes what she looks like, and what kind of a life she has. I wonder about these things, but I don't have enough curiosity to go seek her out.

Q: Do you think it's a mistake for adoptive parents to refer to the birth mother as the woman who gave you birth or as the "mother"? In other words, what would you advise on terminology that would be less confusing to a child?

A: I think originally if the child was told when he was very young, as I was told, I would refer to her as a woman. Because if you start by referring to her as "your mother," the child is going to say, "No, you're my mother, what do you mean?" And I think as they grow older and they understand

a little more, then it is all right to
bring in the concept of the mother. So,
I think it depends on the age of the child.
A three- or four-year-old is too young to
understand the concept of two mothers.
Consequently, I would lean toward referring
to her as the "lady" or "woman." Besides,
it's consistent with the idea that the
mother is the one who brings you up.

Adopted children, as all children, have certain
rights. Dr. Barbara Stilwell, a psychiatrist in private practice, recently delineated these rights most
poignantly for the adopted child.

"I have a right to be wanted . . . by at
least one adult . . . and preferably two. I
want to be wanted very intensely because I have
been rejected at a very tender age . . . for
perhaps a very necessary and even inevitable
reason. Because of that rejection, I am
particularly vulnerable to feelings of dis-
illusionment and abandonment. In order to
develop human trust, I need to feel especially
secure with the generous adults who have chosen
to adopt me.

"I have a right to expediency in adoption
. . . because I desperately need continuity of
care. It will give me a security that will
make my whole development flow more smoothly.
I won't be afraid to grow.

"But don't adopt me before you are ready;
preparation is mandatory before I cross the
threshhold of your home. Part of that preparation is grieving! Yes, grieving the loss of
your procreative function or that of your
spouse's. It's a great loss, you know, like
losing a family member, or a job, or a limb,

51

or some other vital function. It requires
time to absorb the loss . . . time to work
through the various stages of grief; denial,
depression, anger and acceptance. It won't
go smoothly . . . one, two, three, four.
There will be times you think you're over it,
and then you'll cry all the next day. There
will be times you will rage with anger and
blame any source you can think of. There will
be times of numbness and indifference. But
you will work it through . . . and then you'll
be ready to commit yourself to me.

"The other part of preparation is the ex-
citing part. Remember . . . natural parents
have nine months of preparatory excitement. I
expect you to read books, go shopping for baby
furniture, talk your head off and hold every
baby that comes within sight. And, by the time
that phone call comes to tell you I'm on my
way, I expect you to be cool as a cucumber,
because . . .

"I have a right to parents who are free of
overwhelming anxiety. I know you don't know
just how to hold me . . . or how to decipher
my messages of need . . . or how to respond to
my every cry. But you'll learn . . . if
you're confident and committed . . . and have
the support of helping people.

"When you commit yourself to me, I want
you to realize you are taking a risk! I may
not fulfill your fantasies of what a child
should be. Just as I may be bald-headed and
cross-eyed in infancy, I may later show some
real defects that can't be identified in infancy. Remember . . . if I were a natural
child, you would be taking risks, too. With
adoption you are taking a few more. There is
no way I can come to your home with a guarantee

52

of beauty, creative talents and an IQ of 140.
I'm just a human being. I have a right to be
accepted for what I am.

"And if I do turn out to have a major
defect . . . I expect you to grieve . . .
just like any other loss . . . denial, depression, anger, acceptance. It's part of life.

"Do I want to know that I'm adopted? Sure,
when I'm able to understand the information.
I will develop different levels of understanding
at different ages. Make sure you don't give
me more information than I want to know. Brief,
simple answers will always suffice until I ask
another question. And, for goodness sakes,
don't give me that gushy 'chosen child' stuff.
I'm awfully big-headed as a child, anyway. If
you feed me a fantasy that I am 'special,' I'll
think I deserve unlimited privileges and may
behave like a real 'monster.' It will be much
harder for me to contain my aggression if I
think I'm a 'privileged character.'

"Many children have fantasies that they
have another set of parents somewhere who are
superhuman beings. They 'give presents, never
discipline and never say no to anything.' These
fantasies arise when a child becomes angry at
his parents. They dissipate when a child learns
that he can love and hate the same person. As
an adopted child I may prolong this fantasy because the first half of it is true. I do have
a 'real' mom and dad somewhere. If my parents
don't rear me with realistic limit setting and
help me keep my feelings about love and hate
integrated, I'll make that fantasy grow as tall
as the biggest windmill.

"The flip side of that fantasy record is
that I'm a no-good reject. It carries such

53

imagery as 'my mother was a slut and my father
a runaway drunken bum.' If I rely on that
imagery, I don't ever have to expect much from
myself . . . because I was never anything worthwhile to begin with. As an adoptive parent you
must be calm about my background and rear me
with positive attitudes and messages. If you
are uneasy about my background and continuously
see the 'evil' in me, I'll develop an imperme-
able, negative self-concept that no psychothera-
peutic sledgehammer can crack. I must learn
that I am a summation of all my experiences, not
just my genealogical roots.

"And when the age of maturity comes . . .
and I have an interest in my genealogical roots,
I have the right to pursue them. My young adult
ego strives for identity; I have a right to a
sense of history in working out that identity.
Camouflage and intrigue build fantasies; truth
builds a sense of reality.

"I need parents who have a deep respect for
each other. Like natural children, I will
develop oedipal strivings. I'll have times of
wanting an exclusive relationship with my parent
of the opposite sex and a desire to force my
same-sexed parent out of the relationship. If
my parents' marriage is in jeopardy, that fantasy
may come too close to coming true. I must not
be used by one parent to control the other. I
am not a channel of communication. I have no
childhood degree in family relations. I cannot
come into a home to solve marital strife. I
need parents who know how to love each other.

"I need parents who can share their love
with me. Some parents are too exclusive with
their love. I know an adopted girl who felt
so rejected by her parents' love for each other

54

that her greatest desire was to have a baby so she could create her own loving relationship. Other adolescents turn to a sexual relationship too soon out of the same motivation. I need a parent-child relationship that is as loving as the marital relationship.

"I have a right to be loved just for myself . . . not because I am a banner of social cause. If I am interracial, I want to grow up in an environment that will tolerate me with my mixed identity. I want to be around others who are like me. I am not an issue; I am a person. I need a community of friends who will accept me.

"I do not want to be an experiment for parents who may have failed in previous parenting experiences. I have a right to parents who are free of mental illness. I cannot be a cure for someone's neurosis.

"Lastly, I have a right to parents who keep on growing. When the adoption is 'closed', the job has just begun. I have a right to parents who will counsel, read, attend classes and do everything possible to keep in tune with my developmental expectations and needs. I need parents who will get me help if I need it, without feeling they have failed. My psychological growth is made more complex by adoption, and I want every opportunity to grow up healthy, happy and proud."*

*From an address given by Barbara Stilwell, M.D., titled "The Emotional Rights and Needs of the Adopted Child -- As Voiced by a Child" on April 20, 1976, at a symposium titled "Major Dilemmas in Neonatal Pediatrics."

In attempting to relate your feelings of love to the child, as well as your presumed understanding of the birth parents' motivation to release the child for adoption, it is best to convey your own understanding of the nature of love. The notion of "love at first sight" is undoubtedly a myth in most instances. The child should not be taught that love in any relationship occurs instantaneously. Love is something that is nurtured and deepens as people live and share meaningful experiences with each other.

It may be difficult to discuss adoption with a child without implying that he was rescued from inadequate parents. The difficulty arises, in part, from the problems adoptive parents who wanted a child so badly themselves have in identifying with parents who relinquish their child. Birth parents must be accepted for themselves as people, without judgment for their actions, lest criticism of them gives the child the impression that he, too, is being criticized. The perception of unacceptability must be changed through assurances that the child is, indeed, wanted. The most important thing for adoptive parents to recognize is that the child wants to know not how he got here, but whether his parents are glad that he is here.

The adopted child must be assured there are positive as well as negative aspects of his situation. His feelings of loss and rejection can be countered by stressing his desirability and goodness. Certainly, the recognition that he was and is wanted can lead him to a healthy self-concept.

CHAPTER VI

THE MEANING OF ADOPTION TO THE ADOLESCENT

In reviewing the literature on the psychology of adolescence, one fact emerges clearly: Adolescence is a troublesome time of life when self-doubts and searching questions are the rule rather than the exception. For the adopted child, problems encountered in adolescence can make the search for self-identity even more difficult, particularly if the child's relationship with his parents is strained.

Generally, the period of adolescence is fraught with ambivalence. For all children, biological and adopted, this time is the beginning of the end of parental domination. As parental control diminishes, however, the child is called on to respond with increased responsibility for his own decision-making. And, this new role can cause the child considerable anxiety. Added to the stress is the mystique and intrigue regarding romance, which emerges during adolescence. Actual or imagined sexual experiences bring apprehension as well as pleasure.

This is a time of life that should be viewed as a transitional period of development rather than as behavior that remains fixed. Adolescence is essentially an in-between stage, with no special rights and privileges of its own, and which forms the basis of the need to examine and reexamine, in a very real sense, for the first time, what the individual's purpose and destiny in life is apt to be.

Certain characteristics typical of adolescence include the following:

(1) The adolescent is struggling for independence, vehemently protesting against the protective rulings of the adult group. On the other

57

hand, he is unable to handle his independence as well as he did in the pre-adolescent period. He is apt to make the kind of demands for dependent security which have not been made since he was a small child.

(2) The peer group dominates his thinking and his behavior. Violation of peer group rules is extremely difficult for the adolescent.

(3) His verbalizations and his actual behavior are, from day to day, characteristically contradictory. He seems to be an idealist and, yet, his behavior does not always bear this out. At one time he too rigidly follows an idealized code of conduct, and then, as if by a sudden metamorphosis of character, he violates -- or more often talks of violating -- every acceptable code of behavior.

(4) His relationship with other people is confusing. One moment he hates, the next he loves. The object of this emotional response may be the same person or it may be a different person.

(5) He alternates between rejection and idealization of his parents. First, he rejects them outright. In almost the next breath, he idealizes them.

(6) He is characteristically secretive about himself and his feelings but, on the other hand, may bare his soul (or so it seems), revealing dreams, guilt and conflict.

(7) Body changes are extremely rapid because of the excessive hormonal changes, and this contributes to a feeling of body strangeness.

According to Erik Erikson, a noted analyst, the establishment of a sense of identity is the foremost task facing the adolescent (1950). Self-identity is viewed by the adolescent as something precious -- it tells him who he is, how he came into being and what his role in society is to be. He asks himself, "Am I a child or an adult?", "Will I be a good spouse and parent someday?", "Will my race, religion or background prevent me from achieving my goals?" and "Will I be a success or a failure?" Because of the many questions he may pose for himself, the adolescent is sometimes obsessively preoccupied with how he appears in the eyes of others as compared with his own self-image. According to Erikson, failure to achieve a sense of identity leads to identity diffusion, a feeling of not really knowing who one is.

If adolescents living with their biological parents suffer from a crisis identity, the confusion faced by the adopted child is compounded by the fact that he has been exposed to the knowledge that he does have birth parents. The genealogical questions become paramount as he learns about reproduction and childbearing, particularly at a time in our history when there is heightened awareness of the genetic aspects of functioning, as, for example, his intellectual endowment. Reactions to adolescence may vary, as it will in all adolescents. He may deny the existence of some traits he believes are inherited. The degree to which he works out such conflicts is directly related to the success the adoptive parents have had in conveying the message that while he was given up by his birth parents, it was not because of anything he did or did not do, but because of the circumstances in which they found themselves.

The adolescent adoptee has a legitimate right to question his ancestral roots. Such questioning does not imply that the parents have somehow failed the child. It is characteristic of all adolescents,

59

adopted <u>and</u> biological, to question and even reject parental standards in preference to peer standards. This behavior should be viewed with the calm willingness to discuss anything of concern to the adolescent. Keeping the lines of communication open is vital to healthy resolution of some of the universal interpersonal tensions characteristic of the adolescent years.

If the adolescent has questions about genetic or hereditary characteristics, and if the adoptive parents have access to such knowledge, the information should be made available to the adoptee. Generally, the adolescent is curious about what his birth parents looked like and what kind of lifestyles they led rather than names, place and date of birth, etc.

Ultimately, conflicts do arise and tension is inevitable. Arguments over whether the adoptive or birth parents are the "real" parents can be used as a weapon by either the adolescent or the parent. Children may use any weapons available to them in battles with their parents. The adopted child simply has one more in his arsenal. When the adolescent strikes out angrily, saying, "I don't have to listen to you, you aren't my real parents anyway," the most appropriate response may be to let it drop without further comment (but not give in). Then, when cooler heads prevail, comment on the use made by your adolescent of the fact of adoption. You might then say, "We have cared for you as if you were our birth child and our feelings for you are the same as if you were born to us. We will not let you use the adoption as a way to control us. We don't use it and we don't feel it is fair for you to use it." Such communication lets the adolescent know that his feelings are understandable and that his relationship with his parents is a special one. The message reaffirms that he is, indeed, the adopted parents' child.

The handling of such volatile situations is extremely important. Resolution of such issues, in our point of view, depends upon the preexisting nature of the relationship between adoptive parents and their children. It is crucial that such a potentially explosive situation be handled with honesty and sincerity. By adolescence, the child's power of perception is acute. Because adolescents are sensitive to mixed messages, insincerity and hypocrisy, it is vital that the adoptive parent recognize his own feelings before attempting to re-assure the child about his origins. The common practice of referring to the birth parents as "good people" from respectable families who, because of age and general immaturity, put the needs of the child before their own needs and gave him up for adoption may provide the child with a respectable pedigree, but it also feeds into the family romance fantasy discussed earlier. If such a story is essentially untrue, the child can usually sense the dishonesty and the relationship between the adoptive parent and the child may be irreparably damaged rather than strengthened. The admonition "know thyself" is ever so true in dealing with the adolescent adoptee.

Adopters invariably ask child care experts about adoptees' searches for their birth parents. Parents should realize that interest on the part of their children to find out more about their heritage may be a function of mixed and often multiple motivations. Some are curious only about looks and physical characteristics of birth parents, as well as disease proneness. Others are obsessed with the notion that their genetic forebears, and their interest is tied to a need to determine one's psychological identity. Parents should recognize that it is only natural for adolescents to wonder about who they look like and, having missed out on this opportunity, to once again ask the question, "Why?"

61

As stated earlier, the sealed record controversy is one of the most hotly debated issues in
contemporary child caring practices. There are
legal and constitutional questions involved, centering
once again on the "equal protection" clause and other
passages of the Constitution of the United States.
The legalities of the issue have resulted in a modified view of sound adoption practices. In December
of 1976, the Child Welfare League of America, the
national standard-setting agency in the child welfare
field, expressed a modified view. The League re-
affirmed its belief in the principle of confidentiality
as a value to the birth parents, adoptee and adoptive
parents. It recognized, however, that firm and abso-
lute assurances of confidentiality over an extended
period of time may not be realistic. Inasmuch as
there is mounting pressure to change the laws regarding
anonymity and confidentiality (with respect to birth
records), the day may come when an adoptee, in a
given state, will exercise the right to learn of the
identity of his birth parents (1976).

There are some alternative positions currently
held by all those involved in the sealed adoption
record controversy. Those who believe adopted persons
have an unconditional right to know their biological
backgrounds seek to change existing policy on constitutional grounds. They would advocate giving the
adoptee such information at whatever age it is re-
quested, with no conditions attached. Those who believe it is paramount to protect the confidentiality
and anonymity surrounding the adoption process, and
that opening up adoption records would cause little
good and much harm, hold firmly to the status quo.

A third group, believing that adoptees have a
qualified right to know, seeks to balance the rights of
adopted persons against those of birth parents and
those of adoptive parents. One suggestion advocated
involves the establishment of a mediating board which

would review requests for adoption records from adoptees upon their reaching the age of majority and would release the information only upon receiving the permission of the adoptive parents and the birth parents.

On the point of the search, parents should recognize that their children have a right to question. Parents should view the questioning with an open mind and identify with the child's curiosity by indicating the naturalness of such questioning. The adoptive parent should not (one might even say must not) interpret the adolescent's questions as a rejection of them as parents. Depending on the nature of the questions for which the adoptee is seeking answers, our advice is to let the child know that, "Such questions are universal and that they are welcome matters for discussion. If they are questions about physical and medical characteristics, we can provide you with these data to the extent that we have them. If, on the other hand, you actually want and need to find this person (or persons), we will, at the time of your majority, assist you in any way possible. But it is a difficult decision and we will support you in any decision that you make. If finding this woman or man will result in answering these questions for you, we are all in favor of it. But you should wait until you are ready, and you should be ready to accept the consequences of such an encounter. In other words, if you met the woman who delivered you, think through ahead of time what you would actually say to her." This position gives the adoptee the freedom to make his or her own decision.

An interview with a young adult adoptee, focusing largely on her recollection of her own adolescence, serves to dramatize the points contained thus far.

Q: Do you think growing up as an adoptee is harder than growing up as a nonadoptee?

63

A: I'm not sure. I don't think so.

Q: You don't think there's any difference?

A: There's a difference, but I'm not sure it's any more difficult. There are just some different things you have to work through as far as people not understanding what adoption is, but as far as the normal development that everyone goes through, I don't think I was affected in any negative way or that it is any more difficult.

Q: When you say there are some things to work through, could you elaborate on that?

A: You are a little different, and nobody likes to be different from anyone else. So, you have to understand that, yes, I am different, but it's not necessarily bad to be different. In my instance, I think it was very good to be different. It was a very positive thing to be adopted and that's how it was always viewed. Now, that's not always the case. Some of the kids I ran into who found out that they were adopted associated something bad or negative with that.

Q: Is part of the difference having to deal with the sense that one was once given up?

A: I didn't think of it that way until I was a teen-ager. I just never thought of it in that sense until I really understood what childbearing was all about. I wondered why, but I just left it.

Q: You don't remember asking your parents the question "why"?

64

A: No. I think implicitly it was understood, but I don't ever recall asking the question, except facially or nonverbally. When they said something about adoption, I thought maybe I had a question mark on my face and they would say someone thought we could take better care of you than he or she could. But, actually, in terms of an explicit question, no, that didn't happen. I just accepted it, and I remember hearing that at a pretty young age.

Q: My impression of you is that you are, essentially, a healthy person, you have good peer relationships and that you have developed a fairly good sense of your own personal and social competence. In other words, it strikes me that you have a pretty good view of yourself and that you think of yourself in basically positive terms. Has it always been that way?

A: No. It's had its ups and downs. I feel good about myself when I'm in tune with other people. Other people are very important to me; and, if I'm isolated or feel all alone or I'm not very happy, then I don't feel so good. In those cases, I might be tempted to feel sorry for myself and say "somebody dumped me," or words to that effect. Other times I was angry with my parents and I didn't feel good. I'm not sure that that would be any different than what goes on in the life stages of all people. At times, we all wonder if we are really okay or not. I think as I got older my confidence has increased. There were some things not related to adoption. Our family moved a lot when I was young and that doesn't help when you really don't have anyplace to call home. You're always having to make new friends. That can be a negative experience.

For a while, I got sick of being the new
kid. That really didn't have anything to
do with adoption, and it's hard for me to
separate that out. And, finally, when we did
settle in one neighborhood, that's when I
really began feeling like, yes, this is a
home. We were closer to being a family at
that point.

Q: So, in general, you think that the self-
concept a person has, his feelings about himself as a worthwhile person, may or may not
have anything to do with adoption?

A: Well, I think it can have a great deal to
do with it. I've seen other children who
in these instances were not told until very
late in life, and it really undermined everything that they thought about themselves and
their parents. For me, being told at the very
beginning, it was just a given. And the attitude was: This is the way we live, this is
what we live with and that's the way it is.
So, in that instance, I think it's something
you accept, like the color of your hair and
the color of your eyes. You grow with it.
You grow up with the idea that you are adopted

Q: I take it that you are talking about infant
adoption, and I'm assuming that you were
adopted when you were an infant.

A: Yes.

Q: You may know that there is some controversy
going on right now about the word "chosen".
What, from your point of view, do you think
is desirable? Do you think the word "chosen"
carries with it some implicit messages and
what effect do you think this has on the child

66

A: It was used with me, and it was recommended, I believe at the time, by whoever was involved with my parents. It was used in the form that "we were able to choose you." It made me feel very special.

Q: That anything you did was okay? Is that what you mean?

A: Yes, but my parents were tempering that with me.

Q: You knew that there were limits?

A: Oh, yes.

Q: And you knew what those limits were?

A: But I think it can be used in a number of ways, some of which may turn out to be to the child's detriment. I don't think that was the case with me, but it might have been. I do remember asking myself or wondering why I was so special and chosen. I still knew that there were definite boundaries. I was never allowed to behave just in any way I wanted to, but I also knew I was a special thing to them and they had chosen me in every sense of the word.

Q: In one sense. In another sense, somebody chose you for them. They weren't the ones who did the choosing.

A: Well, now, that's interesting. They told me that when they were allowed to go into the nursery and look at all the children and when my dad-to-be picked me up, I pulled on his tie; so, there was much more of a choosing process connected with this.

Q: I see. There were several infants around?

A: Now, that's what I'm not understanding.
Whether somebody actually handed me to them
or whether they could see others, I'm not
really sure. I never clarified that. I
remember the story being told several times,
and I never pinned them down exactly as to
whether there were three or four or five
other infants crawling around. I don't know
how it really happened, but the way it was
told to me, in a way, was that I chose my
parents by pulling on the tie. Maybe it's
gotten more rosy in their memories as the
years have gone by.

Q: Perhaps that is a good example of the "blue
ribbon" concept baby. Because infant adoption in those days was considerably easier,
it was only the most fit of all the children
who were the survivors, in a sense. Those
were also the days of delayed placement, I
take it?

A: Yes, I was almost six months old when my parents adopted me. So, they missed a whole lot
of my real early development; and, so, they
tried to share with me all of the things they
could remember from the time they had me.

Q: But really, in truth, the word "wanted" is
more to the point, and I think that's what,
really, a lot of people have in mind when they
react to the business of being "chosen". For
instance, in a family where there are both
adopted children and biological children, the
word "chosen" would not be the most appropriate term to use. What would this mean in
terms of the biological children? So, maybe
the word "wanted" is more appropriate and,

68

certainly, "wanted" is implied in the word "chosen."

Any fantasies that you can share with me about your birth parents?

A: I'm not sure these are fantasies or just thoughts, but my parents said that my original mother did wear glasses. I guess I would like to believe that she was fairly intelligent, had fair coloring like my own, and I guess I would like to believe that she really wanted me but just couldn't handle the responsibility. I always think of her as an older woman.

Q: Older?

A: Yes, maybe 30 to 35. Never as a young woman.

Q: Was she explained to you that way?

A: No. There was no age mentioned, no reference as to whether she was a teen-ager or in her 20's. I just always think that way; maybe because my own mother was in her 30's by the time I was adopted. Other than that, I really can't remember, but once in a while I do wonder what she might have looked like.

Q: How about the birth father?

A: I have an image of him, too, and I think, for some reason, and maybe it's because of my own close association with my adoptive dad, who I consider my dad, that I might like to meet him. I don't know why not my original mother, but for some reason I have an inkling that someday maybe I will meet him. But I don't know what I would say if I did meet him.

Q: This is interesting, because I think the
    fantasy most of us have is that the birth
    father is viewed strictly as a necessary,
    but relatively unimportant, partner.

A: For some reason, I don't think of him as
    totally uninvolved. My fantasy is that there
    was a close relationship. Whether or not it
    might have led to marriage is something I
    often wonder about.

Q: Is there a sense of loss that occurs some-
    where along the line?

A: I'm not sure, consciously, but just from
    what I understand of my own behavior, which
    is hard to be objective about, I can say
    this: Friends mean a lot to me, and people
    mean a lot to me. And death is very signifi-
    cant to me, like I really feel it. Whether
    that is a carry-over from a previous sense
    of loss or not, I don't know. I do know that
    I am so tuned in to the possibility of losing
    people, so much that sometimes I don't allow
    myself to get too close to them if I know
    they're going to be gone fairly soon. But
    as far as any other symptom, like grieving,
    I cannot say.

Q: Is adolescence harder for an adoptee?

A: I think so, a little. I don't know about
    male adoptees, but I have struggled with the
    question, "Do I tell my boyfriends or don't
    I?", especially if I've been dating them
    for a while and especially if the relation-
    ship may lead to marriage. When do I tell
    them is the question, and I believe I came
    to understand how my mother must have felt
    not to be able to have children. I was able

70

to sympathize with her. Also, you are recognizing how children came into the world at that time of development, so it opens up that whole area of sexuality and childbearing.

Q: Did the term "illegitimacy" bother you?

A: Yes, because I didn't know about my own beginnings and I felt people made judgments about me because of the circumstances into which I was born, and I didn't think that was right. Yes, it does bother me, although not to the extent that it once did.

Q: Well, it would seem to me that if you're pretty clear on who you are this should not be that troublesome an issue. If you know who you are, then, it would appear that you get your sense of who you are in relation to the clarity of the communication from your parents that you are one of them.

A: Yes, and this became important with the extended family, and I was never singled out as "our adopted daughter" or "granddaughter". So, how the extended family deals with the adoption issue is very important.

Q: As you know, there is a controversy over the sealed record of the child's birth. Does that do anything to you? You know, the business of a conflict of rights between the adoptee, the birth parents and the adoptive parents?

A: I've done some research of my own on that question, and I don't have one set answer. That's why I don't think there can be one set policy to govern all situations. I wish, ideally, every case could be looked at on its

own merits and on a case-by-case basis. I
realize there may be overwhelming needs on
the part of the adoptee to find out, but I
don't feel that people who don't want to be
contacted or disturbed should have these wishes
violated. One of the suggestions is a mediating board which can act as a screening de-
vice for both the adoptee and the birth parent.
If both independently desire a contact, the
mediating board can be the means for such a
meeting. That sounds great, but if it were
a situation in which I were contacted by a
board and told that one of my birth parents
wanted to see me, then I would have to play
the "heavy" and say "no." That would be an
awful infringement. In practice, it is a
very difficult situation to set out a uniform
policy that works to everyone's satisfaction
in all cases.

Q: Well, it is an awfully perplexing problem,
to be sure, and I'm not sure there is any way
to reconcile the conflicting rights of all
parties concerned, because one of the givens
at the time of the adoption is that this was
a final decision, this was irrevocable, and
that no biological parent went into this
contract thinking that sometime in the
future he or she would be approached by someone who said, "I know who you are." It is
viewed as a final step, a break with the past,
and having made this decision, he or she
is in a position to put the pieces to his or
her life back together and resume, as much
as possible, a normal life.

A: I agree, totally, and it's also a break for
the adoptive parents.

Q: Do you think adoptees have a greater sense of
gratitude to their parents than nonadoptees?

72

A: Yes.

Q: Do you?

A: I really do; and, for a while, I thought it was a problem for me and my marriage, because I am so devoted to my parents. Of course, being an only child doesn't aid that any, but that's why I leveled with my husband before I married him. I said, "This is the way it is." The pull is definitely there. I know they gave me a lot, but then I look at my husband and I know his parents gave him a lot, too. So, in retrospect, I'm not really sure I can answer that question in any definitive manner.

Q: I can understand that because one can speak only from his or her own standpoint. An adoptee cannot really state what his feelings for his parents might be if he were a biological child, and a biological child cannot really know what his feelings might be if he or she were adopted.

A: I suppose you can say that they are responsible for a lot of what I am; but my looks, anything that is hereditary, they weren't responsible for. The whole nature-nurture question is one that fascinates me. While I like to give my adoptive parents all the credit, there are parts of me that are attributable to my genes.

Q: Well, I happen to know you are quite gifted and, so, while you came with something, they nurtured it.

A: Definitely; and in a different environment, it might not have been.

73

Q: One final question: Is there something you
   think adoptive parents ought to know in
   rearing a child they adopted?

A: They really have an opportunity to explore
   a different avenue in life and that it can
   be as rewarding an experience as natural
   parenthood. It's still parenting, and
   that is what is important, in spite of the
   differences. It is still the relationship
   that is the key. As far as certain pointers
   are concerned, I would stress honesty --
   total and complete in all things -- and
   especially with an adopted child.

Adolescence, a time of transition from childhood
to adulthood, is always filled with searching anxiety.
Adoptive parents must realize that their adolescent
child faces even greater obstacles in his search for
identity than his nonadopted peers and offer him love,
acceptance and assistance in answering the important
questions he may pose for himself in his search for
identity. Honesty and sincerity must be the parents'
guiding forces if they are to have positive relationships with their adolescent adopted child.

CHAPTER VII

THE UNMARRIED MOTHER

It is not unusual for adopters to wonder about
the birth parents who decided to relinquish parental
rights and place the child for adoption. Questions
surface in the adoptive parents' minds along the
following lines: How did they come to decide on
adoption? How did they feel about their decision?
Was professional help available to them? It is normal
for parents to entertain fantasies about the birth
parents, particularly the woman. Therefore, we feel
this book would not be complete without devoting
appropriate attention to the source of the adoptee --
the unmarried mother.

Traditionally, social agencies have viewed the
unmarried mother's situation, based on their clinical
experience, in a variety of stereotypical ways. The
pregnancy was viewed as an attempted solution to personal or emotional problems. In some cases, the girl's
pregnancy was seen as motivated by an unconscious wish
to punish the parents for being ungiving and unresponsive
to her own needs. In still other cases, the pregnancy
was viewed as an attempt to repair a precarious relationship with her own parents, particularly the mother,
by creating a crisis around which the entire family
could rally. Stereotypically, she is neither promiscuous
nor unfeeling, but does have unresolved personal problems.

Problems exacerbated by the pregnancy result in intense feelings of loneliness, a sense of shame or panic,
a feeling of having betrayed her parents' trust and an
expectation of condemnation. In order to decide upon a
course of action with which she can comfortably live,
she must address these feelings as well as the underlying
conflicts that brought about the pregnancy.

Too often she does not receive adequate assistance.

The physician who treats the unmarried pregnant woman often addresses only her physical needs while neglecting her emotional needs. The failure of many doctors to recognize the emotional aspects of the pregnancy inadvertently and subtly punishes the woman for the dilemma in which she finds herself. The doctor, however, is in a key position to recognize her need for counseling and can, therefore, refer her to appropriate professionals.

The task of counseling is twofold:

(1)   Assisting the woman in verbalizing and accepting her feelings; and

(2)   Helping her make a decision with which she can live for life, taking into account her feelings toward herself, the baby, the putative father and her family.

Her feelings often revolve around concern for the baby and its future, her belief that she has betrayed her parents' trust in her, fantasies about the child's perception of her decision and anger over the circumstances which precipitated her need to make such a difficult and painful decision.

A warm, supportive, nonjudgmental atmosphere will allow the woman to think through her situation and discuss the practical aspects of her planning free from coercion. The counselor who helps the unmarried woman face the thunderous impact of losing a child is responsible for helping her examine her own life as well as the life of her unborn child. This may involve assistance with housing or employment, but, most importantly, involves helping her to identify her strengths and, as she finds satisfaction in making the decision best for herself and the baby, helping her to feel good about herself.

In assisting the woman in decision-making, the counselor must help her to separate fact from fantasy, help her to see the realities involved with raising a child alone and with relinquishing a child she may never see again. Although not always successful in this respect, the counselor who genuinely respects the woman and offers sincere help and understanding during this painful time in her life will become an important support system for the woman.

There have been very few systematic attempts to evaluate the overall effects of the pregnancy and consequent decision-making for the unmarried woman. Evidence is increasingly clear, however, that the unmarried mother feels she is completely alone in an insensitive, uncaring world. Recent research recognizes that even prior to relinquishing the child, perhaps as soon as she first experiences fetal movement, she experiences a grief reaction in anticipation of the loss. The denial of pregnancy, which can be equated with the denial stage characteristic of all mourning reactions, may be experienced in conjunction with the feeling of fetal movement, leading to intensely conflicting emotions.

An interview with a young woman who relinquished her baby for adoption seven years prior to the interview illustrates many of the points that have been mentioned:

Q: Do you think of this child as still your child?

A: Sometimes, but I have to qualify that, because I don't think in terms of this child being my child; I think in terms of having a child who is seven years old somewhere. And, when I think of that child being mine, I think of him only in terms of giving birth to him. Anything else that he has in his life has been from his adoptive parents, so I don't think in terms of him being mine, I guess.

Q: Do you think at some point in his life he might be angry with you?

A: Yes.

Q: Why?

A: Because I think that there will probably be a time when he will really question my motives for giving him up. I think it will be very difficult, because he doesn't know the reasons and because I, obviously, cannot talk to him. But, because he does not know the reasons why I gave him up, then I think there is a possibility that he will see my giving him up as not wanting him, and that is very sad. If there would be a way of preventing those kinds of feelings, it would be real nice.

Q: There are ways of diluting the sense that you gave him up, but that, from my point of view, is very dependent upon how accepting his adoptive parents are of him, that he does have parents who love him. This is probably your fantasy, isn't it, that he has parents who love him and accept him?

A: Right. Oh, I could not think anything else. It would hurt too much.

Q: You referred to the real reasons you gave him up. Could you talk about that a little bit?

A: I was 23 at the time that I had him and I was not married. At the time I found out I was pregnant, I quit my job. I had some money saved up, so finances were not really a problem, but I did not feel I could give him any kind of life that he deserved. While I didn't realize it at the time, I became aware afterwards that during the time I was pregnant I

very much wanted to keep him, but I think
it would have been a very selfish thing for
me to do. I don't know that I would have
been able to give him a very happy life.

Q: So, you're saying, during the time that you
were making this decision about what to do,
there were these mixed feelings?

A: Oh, yes.

Q: That emotionally you may have wanted to keep
him, but realistically you knew this was
going to be the best for him?

A: Right.

Q: Did you get any help professionally during
this phase?

A: I didn't find out for certain that I was pregnant until I was about five months into the
pregnancy, and I talked to a friend of mine
who is a professional and asked him where to
go for help. I pretty much decided right away
that the only thing that I could do was give
the baby up for adoption, so I talked to a
friend of mine, and he recommended this particular agency. I cannot say that I really got
any kind of help, because I was not very honest
about my feelings. I went to my scheduled
appointments, and I talked to this lady and
told her that everything was fine and there
were no problems. I was not in touch with my
feelings at that point, because I was afraid
to be, and I surely wasn't going to let her
help me get in touch with them.

Q: Why not?

A: Because I would have felt overwhelmed.

Q: By the sense of impending loss? Is that what you mean?

A: Impending loss, also anger. Anger because I was pregnant and frightened. I was very ' frightened of just going through the physical changes of being pregnant and the physical things involved in having a baby. I was real scared.

Q: And the worker never picked this up?

A: No. Or, if she did, she wanted to leave it alone. I don't know. I have a feeling that she didn't know it.

Q: Mostly because part of you didn't want her to pick it up. Right?

A: Right.

Q: What are your thoughts now, seven years after placing the baby? You don't know the adoptive couple, I take it?

A: No. I know a few things about them, but I have no idea and no feelings of wanting to find out.

Q: What does this controversy of people looking up their birth parents eighteen to twenty years after they are born do to you?

A: That scares me. I am not sure that I can explain it, but I think it would hurt a great deal just to see my child. To have someone come up to you and say, "You know, I know you're my mother," would be very painful,

80

because all I could think about would be the
fact that he had shown me what I had missed
by not rearing him these past eighteen years,
and in that one split moment I would realize
all that I had missed.

Q: So, you are saying, in effect, that you would
be strongly opposed to any effort to seek you
out. One other question: Is there something
you think that parents ought to know in raising
the child who is theirs by the adoptive process?

A: I can't really think of anything except for
one thing. I don't know how much adoptive
parents are told about the parents of the
child, the mother of the child, but it is very
important to me that adoptive parents realize
that mothers do hurt when they are giving up a
child. It is not something that is done in a
callous moment, but done only after much
thinking and consideration of all of the alternatives having been weighed very carefully.

Unmarried parents are not of a single kind. There
is no typical case. Frankly, we do not know how representative this woman's views are of those who have relinquished a baby for purposes of adoption. One study does
suggest that thoughts about the child do linger (Sorosky,
Baran and Pannor, 1979). But, this dialogue does high-
light some of the most common concerns voiced by unmarried mothers and shows the birth mother's typical
sensitivity toward the child.

CHAPTER VIII

RESEARCH FINDINGS

Everyone is interested in knowing what makes for
a successful adoption. Professionals in the field
are interested in the salient factors which contribute
to successful adoption in order to effectively evaluate, select and counsel prospective adoptive couples.
The adoptive parents are interested because they want
to handle special problems related to adoption in a
way that will contribute positively to their children's
social and emotional development. The children, themselves, want to receive good parenting, as do all
children.

Nevertheless, it is not surprising that there have
only been few systematic attempts to examine the impact
of adoption itself or current adoption practices upon
the development of the child. The methodological
problems are enormous. It is difficult, if not impos-
sible, for the researcher to isolate the factor of
adoptive status from all the other factors affecting a
child's adjustment. A standard research text (Kerlinger,
1964) presents the problem quite succinctly:

> It is not always possible for a researcher
> to formulate his problem simply, clearly and
> completely. He may often have only a rather
> general, diffuse, even confused notion of the
> problem. This is in the nature of the complex-
> ity of scientific research (p. 18).

One of the major problems posed for the researcher
is the effort to obtain a large and representative sample
of adopted children and families. They are difficult to
locate because they have been guaranteed anonymity and
confidentiality by those involved in arranging the adoption. Even if they are located, not every adopter or
adoptee will agree to be a subject for study. For many,

adoption remains a sensitive issue which they are un-
comfortable in discussing. One cannot assume, therefore, that those who do cooperate with the researcher
are representative of all adoptees or adopters.
Further, the ethics of research require that we do
not violate promises made earlier or stir up old
issues or subjects which might hurt people and which
people request that we leave alone.

Thus, the multiplicity of the interrelated variables and limitations in the sample itself present
formidable problems in ferreting out the myriad
factors associated with success or failure in adoption.
They pose problems of interpretation of the presently
available data. They also present formidable obstacles
in obtaining answers to questions of interest to those
in the adoption field. In brief, the lot of the researcher is to rule out alternative explanations for
the phenomenon under investigation. To put it another
way, he must convince himself that what he thinks is
responsible for the occurrence of the phenomenon is
truly responsible and not something else.

There has been considerable speculation that the
adopted child is more prone to develop psychiatric
problems. The evidence supporting this alleged vulner-
ability is that adoptees are disproportionately represented in caseloads of mental health practitioners.
There are several methodological problems frequently
overlooked in the interpretation of such findings, not
the least of which is the fact that certain coincidental
socio-cultural differences between adopted and nonadopted families are overlooked.

(1)   The problem of self-selection is a limiting
      factor in properly evaluating research re-
      sults. The problem of self-selection is
      that when people are drawn into a sample
      because they possess a particular character-
      istic (in this case, adoption), what is

overlooked is the fact that these same
people possess other traits or characteristics of which the investigator is unaware;

(2) Adoptive families tend to be well-educated,
upper-middle class and success-oriented.
Having sought out an agency (or other professionals) to obtain a child, they are
more likely to seek the services of professionals whenever the situation calls for it;
and

(3) In the various adoptive studies, there is a
variation in the actual measures, the cri-
teria for evaluating adoptive outcome and
the methodology employed. Among the list
of outcome measures are parental satisfaction, parental ratings of the child's interpersonal adjustment, academic performance
and the quality of the parent-child relationship. Variation in the methodology includes the methods used in obtaining data,
sources of data, types of samples used and
statistical measures used in analyzing outcome.

While it is true that a disproportionate number
of adoptees are seen in psychiatric clinics, the vast
majority of them are not. Kadushin, a nationally recognized child welfare researcher, noted that 98% of adopted
children have never been referred for psychiatric treat-
ment (1966). Further, those cases selected on a random
basis, or through one of a matching procedure (to insure
comparability of groups), suggest few differences, if
any, between adopted and nonadopted populations. It
would appear that on the face of it adoptees are seen
with greater frequency than one would expect. On the
other hand, a number of studies which used larger samples and accepted scientific procedure for analyzing

results demonstrate that, with few exceptions, adopted children develop as physically and emotionally stable as their nonadopted peers. One might even entertain the idea that differences in methodology result in differences in outcome. Nevertheless, certain findings have contributed significantly to our understanding of adoption, and it might be helpful to examine more closely differences between families who do require professional help and those who do not. For those who do receive services related to adoption, there are a variety of reasons:

(1) Problems of unresolved infertility (e.g., "I still can't help feeling resentful whenever I see a pregnant woman.");

(2) Problems revolving around entitlement (e.g., "I keep asking myself if I have a right to him.");

(3) Problems of the parents' disappointment over growth and development issues; and

(4) Problems inherent in learning of a diagnosis of neurological or intellectual impairment.

These difficulties may play themselves out in the parent-child relationship with the result that the parents are viewed as overprotective and over-defensive in regard to handling the child.

There may be another group whose difficulties are not related to adoption but, because the child is adopted, it is easy for the nonresearch-oriented clinician to blame the difficulty on the fact of adoption. In this category fit the myriad situations in which communication among family members is contradictory, dishonest and destructive. Parents who use their children as pawns for fighting with each other invariably produce a situation in which the children become troubled and, therefore, come to the attention of those in the mental health field. It would seem, then, that the greater incidence of emotional disturbances is not related to the adoption, per se, but to consequent difficulties in the parent-child relationship.

Having cautioned the reader against drawing hasty conclusions based on the interpretation of existing findings, we may now proceed to examine some studies which may be of interest to adoptive parents. One example of an interesting study is that of Triseliotis (1973), a psychiatric social worker in Scotland. In this study, he interviewed seventy adult adoptees, all of whom searched for their birth parents, which is perfectly legal in Scotland.

A detailed review of this group revealed that the adoptive parents, as a whole, violated the prescriptive standard of adoption practice regarding telling. Nearly two-thirds of the children first learned about the adoption when they were eleven years of age or older, and, when they did find out, the source was very likely to be someone other than the adoptive parents. Age of learning about adoption was associated with satisfaction in their relationship with their parents, with the younger-age children expressing the greatest satisfaction and the older-age children the least satisfaction. For those over ten years of age, revelation of adoption was perceived as a shock, requiring a new orientation of the self, concomitant with intense anger at their adoptive parents. The reader should realize, however, that this was a biased sample and not one from which to draw generalizations to all adoptees. In spite of this shortcoming, the research points out the importance of many of the points made earlier in our book about how adoptees should be told, the age of telling and by whom they should be told.

In many respects, the Triseliotis findings are mirrored by those of Sorosky, Baran and Pannor in a series of publications (1978). They studied reunions between adoptees and birth parents as a result of contacts solicited through newspaper accounts of their interest. They, too, experienced revelation concerning adoption relatively later in life and learned about the adoption by someone other than their parents in one-third of the cases. Most of them, as in the case of the Triseliotis study, saw the reunion with their birth parents as advantageous. Most reported a sense of closure and completeness in regard to identity issues. Most saw the reunion as beneficial and none saw it as an attempt to replace their adoptive parents. Rather, they reported, as a result of the meeting, a deeper sense of love for their adoptive parents who they viewed as their "psychological parents."

It is a consistent finding that females are much more likely to engage in the search than are males. It is interesting to speculate on what might be the causes of this phenomenon. There may be some valid explanations for this distribution, however. It may be that the women, as future childbearers, are more sensitive to the issue of discontinuity of the biological line. Another explanation may be the fact that, in our society, women may be more encouraged to express their true feelings about identity concerns. It is not that men do not share such concerns, but their overt expression may be less acceptable than for women.

Most of the evidence suggests that adoptees, by and large, adjust fairly well, suggesting an overreaction to the issue of adoptive status. Kadushin, in

summarizing the findings of eleven outcome studies,
states that 74% had been judged "unequivocably
successful"; 11% were "fairly successful"; and 15%
were "unsatisfactory" (1970). A number of variables,
previously thought to have a bearing on outcome and,
therefore, became major issues in agency adoption
practice, proved to have no basis in fact. These
include: Background factors in the child, the age
of adoptive parents, length of marriage, income, education, socioeconomic status and religion. Matching,
an inviolable cardinal principle of adoption work,
bears no relationship to outcome. The principal factors seem to be parental attitudes toward the child
-- their unconditional acceptance of him and the
degree to which they have worked through feelings of
entitlement.

It seems rather evident that telling is the most
problematic of all the situations for the adopters.
Unfortunately, the available research to date offers
no clear picture of how to best tell a child of his
origins. We believe, however, based for the most part
on our findings, that the age-old practice of telling
the child while he is young is assuredly advisable,
provided it is not overdone and is not done inappropri-
ately. The evidence is strong that the parent-child
relationship which is one of loving and caring is the
best predictor of the most satisfactory outcome.

CHAPTER IX

A CLOSING NOTE

The building blocks of a successful adoption are
communication, acceptance and a strong, secure sense
of identity. In a close, nurturing family, these
factors emerge together. Communication is perhaps
the most important, because open communication is
necessary for the development of both acceptance
and a sense of identity.

Parents who are able to discuss adoption in a
direct, honest manner teach their children that adoption is acceptable. It is not necessary and, in fact,
it is undesirable that all family communication revolve around adoption. The subject should be neither
dwelled upon nor totally avoided. There is a comfortable middle ground where adoption is acknowledged as a
fact and discussed when it is appropriate. When the
parent continually brings up the adoption in unrelated
conversation, the parent is likely suffering from
unresolved anxieties and will communicate these feelings
to the child. The parent who purposely avoids discussing adoption often harbors unresolved conflicts,
as well, and may unknowingly send his child the message
that adoption is unacceptable. Too much or too little
communication regarding the adoption may cause the
child to question his own desirability and jeopardize
his rightful place within the family unit.

The adopted child and his parents will have
feelings about adoption. The child will likely voice
fears and concerns and ask questions about his adoption from an early age. Parents who acknowledge and
accept their child's feelings put their child on the
road to developing a healthy self-identity. And
parents who answer their child's questions in a direct,
sincere and loving manner teach the child acceptance
of himself and his place in the family situation.

A sense of entitlement is one component necessary
to parental acceptance of the child and the child's
acceptance of himself and his adopted parents. And,
it is natural for the sense of entitlement to develop
over time. The sudden addition of an adopted child
to the family does not magically transform two adults
into parents and a child into a son or daughter.
Often, having waited long for the child, the new parents may feel anxieties as well as excitement and joy
over the new member who is joining the family. It may
take time for them to overcome their reactions to the
initial impact and come to feel that the child is
really, truly theirs.

The ease with which the child accepts his adoptedness is directly related to the degree of success the
adoptive parents have had in accepting their own status
of adoptive parents. Thus, it is imperative for them
to accept their new parenting roles and develop a
sense of entitlement to the child if the child is to
grow up feeling good about himself.

The parents' feelings about infertility can affect
acceptance of their child. Feelings regarding the
inferiority often associated with infertility, and
not the infertility itself, can hinder acceptance of
the child. Hostility can replace love toward the child
if the child is continually viewed as a symbol of
biological inadequacy. Open communication between the
couple and professional counseling may help resolve
feelings about inadequacy. Such counseling toward
resolution of problems associated with infertility
should take place prior to the adoption of the child
whenever possible. Those who come to the realization
that sexual capacity must not be equated with producing
a child can find great emotional satisfaction in their
relationship and in the contribution they can make
to a child's growth and development through adoptive
parenthood.

A child who experiences honest, open communication and feels that his parents accept him becomes an integral part of the family unit. The child feels that he belongs and identifies himself with the family. "The telling" is important to the child's sense of identity. The adoptive parent who assures his child that "you are mine despite the fact that someone else gave birth to you" tells the child that his "real" family is his adoptive family. The child who is taught that adoption is good feels that he, too, is good. He comes to like himself and feels that he is a worthwhile and valuable part of the family. The child comes to see that those who care for and love him, and not those who gave birth to him, are, indeed, his parents.

While adoptees do often encounter difficulties developing a sense of self-identity and resolving the issue of rejection by their birth parents, so do other children, and these factors alone do not put adoptees at greater developmental risk than children living with their biological parents. Vastly more important to the growing child is not the fact of adoption, but the quality of family life in which he finds himself.

Problems are facts of life in even the most loving, accepting families. Families do not always function in harmonious accord. Friction between family members, particularly between children and their parents, must be anticipated and accepted as natural occurrence. It should not be avoided as if it could not or should not exist. For adoptive parents, it may be tempting to attribute parent-child conflict or a child's delayed or inappropriate social behavior to the adoption itself. It is extremely important, and also reassuring, to realize that the most common source of problems are developmental changes which follow a child from infancy to adulthood, not the fact that a child was or was not adopted.

93

Children of adoptive and biological parents face many of the same quandaries, experience many of the same hurts and respond in a similar manner to successes and failures encountered in the process of growing up. They are developing, changing children first. Only secondarily are they biological or adopted sons and daughters. The differences between biological and adoptive children are important. But the numerous and striking similarities are, perhaps, even more important. And the goals of parenthood remain the same, regardless of whether the child joined the family by birth or by adoption.

There are far more similarities than differences between biological and adoptive parenting. Adoption is simply another way of building families, and as such, should be viewed as an accepted way of life. The more people who come to view it this way, the better the opportunities for healthy family growth and communication. The skills, love and caring that go into the formation of solid family ties are the same for all families, regardless of how they came into being.

BIBLIOGRAPHY

Anderson, C. Wilson. "The Sealed Record in Adoption Controversy," Social Service Review, 51, 2 (March, 1977).

Ansfield, Joseph. The Adopted Child. Springfield, Illinois; Charles C. Thomas, Publishers, 1971.

Bettelheim, Bruno. "What Adoption Means To A Child," Ladies Home Journal (October, 1970).

Biskind, Sylvia. "The Group Method in Services to Adoptive Families," Child Welfare, 45, 10 (December, 1969).

Burke, Carolyn. "Adult Adoptee's Constitutional Right To Know His Origins," Southern California Law Review, 48 (May, 1975).

Chestang, Leon. "The Dilemma of Biracial Adoption," Social Work, 17, 3 (May, 1972).

Child Welfare League of America, Standards For Adoption Service; New York: Child Welfare League of America, 1976.

Clothier, Florence. "The Psychology of The Adopted Child," Mental Hygiene, 27 (1943).

Dalsheimer, Babette. "Adoption Runs in My Family," Ms., 2, No. 2 (1973).

Elonen, Anne and Schwartz, Edward. "A Longitudinal Study of the Emotional, Social and Academic Functioning of Adopted Children," Child Welfare, 48 (1969).

Erikson, Erik H. Childhood & Society; New York: Norton & Co., Inc. (1950).

Freud, Sigmund. "Family Romances," Collected Papers, 5; London: Hogarth Press, 1950.

Gochros, Harvey. "A Study of the Caseworker --
  Adoptive Parent Relationship in Postplacement
  Service," Child Welfare, 46 (June, 1967).

Jaffee, Benson. "Adoptive Outcome: A Two Generation
  View," Child Welfare, 53 (April, 1974).

Jaffee, Benson and Fanshel, David. How They Fared in
  Adoption: A Follow-Up Study; New York: Columbia
  University Press, 1970.

Jolowicz, Alameda. "The Hidden Parent: Some Effects
  of Concealment of Parents' Life on the Child's
  Use of Foster Home Care," Source Book of Teaching
  Materials, Child Welfare; New York: Council on
  Social Work Education, 1969.

Kadushin, Alfred. Adopting Older Children; New York:
  Columbia University Press, 1970.

_____. "Adoptive Parenthood: A Hazardous Adventure?",
  Social Work, Vol. 11 (July, 1966).

Kerlinger, Fred. Foundations of Behavior Research;
  San Francisco: Holt, Rinehart & Winston, 1964.

Kirk, H. David. "Community Sentiments in Relation to
  Child Adoption," Unpublished Ph.D. Thesis, Cornell
  University, 1953.

_____. Shared Fate. New York: The Free Press, 1964.

_____. "A Dilemma of Adoptive Parenthood -- Incongruous
  Role Obligation," Marriage and Family Living, 21
  (November, 1959).

Krugman, Dorothy. "Reality in Adoption," Child Welfare,
  43 (July, 1964).

Lawder, Elizabeth A. A Follow-Up Study of Adoptions:
  Postplacement Functioning of Adoption Families;
  New York: Child Welfare League of America, 1969.

Mazor, Miriam D. "Barren Couples," Psychology Today, 13 (May, 1979).

McWhinnie, Alexina. Adopted Children -- How They Grow Up; London: Kegan Paul, Trench, Trubner and Company, 1967.

Mikawa, James and Boston, John. "Psychological Characteristics of Adopted Children," Psychiatric Quarterly Supplement, 42, 2 (July, 1968).

Ripple, Lilian. "A Follow-Up Study of Adopted Children," Social Service Review, 42 (December, 1968).

Schechter, Marshall D. "Observations on Adopted Children," Archives of General Psychiatry, 3 (July, 1960).

Schwartz, Edward M. "The Family Romance Fantasy In Children Adopted In Infancy," Child Welfare, 49 (July, 1970).

Silman, Roberta. Somebody Else's Child; New York: Frederick Warne, 1976.

Sorosky, Arthur, Baran, Annette, and Pannor, Reuben. The Adoption Triangle; Garden City, New York: Anchor Press/Doubleday, 1979.

Triseliotis, John. In Search of Origins; London: Routledge and Kegan Paul, 1973.

Walsh, Ethel and Lewis, Frances. "A Study of Adoptive Mothers In A Child Guidance Clinic," Social Casework, 50, No. 10 (December, 1969).

Ward, Margaret. "The Relationship Between Parents and Caseworker in Adoption." Social Casework, 60 (February, 1979).

97

INDEX